Stories of Success:

The Young Adventurer
(Illustrated)

Stories of Success:

The Young Adventurer
(Illustrated)

Horatio Alger, Jr.

Sumner Books
Hermosa Beach, CA

Stories of Success:
The Young Adventurer (Illustrated)
Copyright © 2015 Sumner Books

FIRST EDITION
Sumner Books
737 3rd St
Hermosa Beach, California 90254
310-337-7003
ISBN 978-1-939104-24-3
CREATORS PUBLISHING

TABLE OF CONTENTS

A NOTE FROM THE PUBLISHER

Once crowned "America's most influential writer," Horatio Alger is hardly known today. Those who are familiar with him think "rags to riches," and that's about it. Most young people have never heard of him.

What an opportunity!

More than a hundred years before our contemporary self-help movement, Horatio Alger paved the way with his vivid illustrations of the keys to success and happiness. Today, Sumner Books is excited to introduce a new generation of Americans to some of the most inspirational stories ever written. Regardless of your age, you simply cannot read a Horatio Alger book without coming away with a good feeling.

Alger's books initially sold in the millions and then the tens of millions and finally the hundreds of millions. In fact, the Chicago Daily News once called Horatio Alger "America's best selling author of all time." Sumner Books is committed to bringing to life this best selling collection in the form of audiobooks read by professional actors and recorded with audio engineers in our studio. Our revised e-books, each with a detailed table of contents and colored illustrations, are professionally edited, including the occasional updating of phrases to make the books as easy to read today as they were when they were first published between 1865 and 1900.

Long after his death in 1899, the magazine Publishers Weekly wrote: "To call Horatio Alger Jr. America's most influential writer may seem like an overstatement ... but ... only Benjamin Franklin meant as much to the formation of the American popular mind."

Our goal is to bring back some of the influence that Alger exerted on millions of young people in America. Yes, it's retro; it's counterintuitive and totally contrary to the cynicism that has become a part of American culture. But we are proud to be leading a movement that is as positive and uplifting as the last pages of a Horatio Alger story.

Rick Newcombe
President
Sumner Books

Stories of Success

"Lucky can often mean simply taking advantage of a situation at the right moment. It is possible to 'make' your luck by being always prepared."
Michael Korda

CHAPTER I

MARK NELSON'S FAMILY

"I wish I could pay off the mortgage on my farm," said Mark Nelson soberly, taking his seat on the left of the fireplace, in the room where his wife and family were assembled.

"Have you paid the interest, Mark?" asked his wife.

"Yes. I paid it this afternoon, and it has stripped me of money completely. I have less than five dollars in my pocket toward buying you and the children clothes for the winter."

"Never mind me," said his wife cheerfully. "I am pretty well provided for."

"Why, mother," said Sarah, the oldest daughter, a girl of fourteen, "you haven't had a new dress for a year."

"I have enough to last me till spring, at any rate," said the mother.

"You never buy anything for yourself."

"I don't go in rags, do I?" asked Mrs. Nelson, with a smile.

Mrs. Nelson had a happy disposition, which led her to accept uncomplainingly, and even cheerfully, the sacrifices which, as the wife of a farmer in poor circumstances, she was compelled to make.

"You are right, Sarah," said Mark Nelson. "Your mother never seems to think of herself. She might have been much better off if she had not married me."

The children did not understand this allusion. They had never been told that their mother had received an offer from Squire Hudson, the wealthiest man in the village, but had chosen instead to marry Mark Nelson, whose only property was a small farm, mortgaged for half its value. Her rejected admirer took the refusal hard, for, as much as it was possible for him, he loved the prettiest girl in the village, as Mary Dale was generally regarded. But Mary knew him to be cold and selfish and could not make up her mind to marry him. If she had done so, she would now be living in the finest house in the village, with the chance of spending the winter in New York or Boston, instead of drudging in a humble home, where there was indeed enough to eat but little money for even necessary purposes. She had never regretted her decision. Her husband, though poor, was generally respected and liked, while the squire, though his money procured him a certain degree of consideration, had no near or attached friends.

To Squire Hudson many in the village paid tribute, for he held mortgages on twenty farms and buildings, and he was strict in exacting prompt payment of the interest semi-annually. It was he to whom Mark Nelson's farm was mortgaged for two thousand dollars. The mortgage had originally been for fifteen hundred dollars, but five years before it had been increased to two thousand, which represented more than half the sum which it would have fetched, if put up for sale. The interest on this sum amounted to a hundred and twenty dollars a year, which Mark Nelson always found it hard to raise. Could he have retained it in his hands and devoted it to the use of his family, it would have helped them wonderfully, with Mrs. Nelson's good management. Tom, the oldest boy, now approaching his sixteenth birthday, looked up from a book he was reading. He was a bright-looking boy, with brown hair, a ruddy complexion and dark-blue eyes, who looked, and was, frank and manly.

"What is the amount of your interest?" he asked.

"Sixty dollars every half-year, Tom. That is what I paid to Squire Hudson this afternoon. It would have made us very comfortable, if I only could have kept it."

"It would have done you more good than the squire," said Sarah.

"He has more money than he knows what to do with," said her father, almost complainingly. "It seems hard that money should be so unevenly distributed."

"Money is not happiness," said Mrs. Nelson quietly.

"No, but it helps to buy happiness."

"I don't think Squire Hudson is as happy a man as you, Mark."

Mark Nelson's face softened as he surveyed his wife and children.

"I am happy at home," he said, "and I don't think the squire is."

"I am sure he isn't," said Tom. "Mrs. Hudson is sour and ill-tempered, and Sinclair -- the only child -- is a second edition of his mother. He is the most unpopular boy in the village."

"Still," said the farmer, not quite convinced, "money is an important element of happiness, and a farmer stands a very poor chance of acquiring it. Tom, I advise you not to be a farmer."

"I don't mean to be if I can help it," said Tom. "I am ready for any opening that offers. I hope some day to pay off the mortgage on the farm and make you a free man, father."

—

"Thank you for your good intentions, Tom, but two thousand dollars is a large sum of money."

"I know it, father, but I was reading in a daily paper, not long ago, of a boy, as poor as myself, who was worth twenty-five thousand dollars by the time he was thirty. Why shouldn't this happen to me?"

"Don't build castles in the air, Tom," said his mother sensibly.

"At least, mother, I may hope for good luck. I have been wanting to talk to you both about my future prospects. I shall be sixteen next week, and it is time I did something."

"You are doing something -- working on the farm now, Tom."

"That don't count. Father advises me not to be a farmer, and I agree with him. I think I am capable of making my way in the world in some other way, where I can earn more money. There is Walter, who likes the country, to stay with you."

Walter, the third child, was now twelve years of age, with decided country tastes.

"I would like to be a farmer as well as anything," said Walter. "I like the fresh air. I shouldn't like to be cooped up in a store, or to live in the city. Let Tom go if he likes."

"I have no objection," said Mr. Nelson, "but I have neither money nor influence to help him. He will have to make his own way."

"I am not afraid to try," said Tom courageously. "From this day I will look out for a chance, if you and mother are willing."

"I shall not oppose your wishes, Tom," said Mrs. Nelson gravely, "though it will be a sad day for me when you leave your home."

"That isn't the way to look at it, mother," said Tom. "If gold pieces grew on currant bushes, it wouldn't be necessary for me to leave home to make a living."

"I wish they did," said Harry, a boy nine years of age.

"What would you do then, Harry?" asked his brother, smiling.

"I would buy a bicycle and a pair of skates."

"I heard of a boy once who found a penny in the field, right under a potato vine," said Walter.

"I don't believe it," said Harry.

"It's true, for I was the boy."

"Where did it come from?"

"Tom put it there to fool me."

—

5

"Won't you put one there to fool me, Tom?" asked Harry.

"You are too smart, Harry," said Tom, laughing. "My pennies are too few to try such experiments. I hope, by the time you are as old as Walter, to give you something better."

The conversation drifted to other topics, with which we are not concerned. Tom, however, did not forget it. He felt that an important question had that evening been decided for him. He had only thought of making a start for himself hitherto. Now he had broached the subject and received the permission of his father and mother. The world was all before him, wherever he chose. His available capital was small, it is true, amounting only to thirty-seven cents and a jack-knife, but he had, besides, a stout heart, a pair of strong hands, an honest face, and plenty of perseverance -- not bad equipment for a young adventurer.

CHAPTER II

TOM FINDS A WALLET

Since the time of which I am writing, over sixty years have passed, for it was in the year 1850 that Tom made up his mind to leave home and seek a fortune. The papers were full of the new gold discoveries in the new country which had recently been added to the great republic. Thousands were hurrying to the land of gold; men who had been unfortunate at home, or, though moderately well situated, were seized by the spirit of adventure. At considerable sacrifice many raised the means of reaching the new El Dorado, while others borrowed or appropriated the necessary sum. Some, able to do neither, set out on a venture, determined to get there in some way.

In the weekly paper, to which Mr. Nelson had for years been a subscriber, Tom had read a good deal about California. His youthful fancy had been wrought upon by the brilliant pictures of a land where a penniless man might, if favored by fortune, have financial security within twelve months, and he ardently wished that he, too, might have the chance of going there. It was a wish, but not an expectation. It would cost at least two hundred dollars to reach the Pacific coast, and there was no hope of getting a tenth of that sum.

An advertisement for sailing to California during the Gold Rush, 1850s.

"If I could only go to California," thought Tom, "I would make my way somehow; I would cheerfully work twelve hours a day. I don't see why a boy can't dig gold as well as a man. If somebody would lend me money enough to get there, I could afford to pay high interest."

There was one man in Wilton who might lend him the money if he would. That man was Squire Hudson. He always had money on hand in considerable quantities, and two hundred dollars would be nothing to him. Tom would not have dreamed of applying to him, however, but for a service which just at this time he was able to render the squire.

Tom had been in search of huckleberries -- for this was the season -- when, in a narrow country road, not much frequented, his attention was drawn to an object lying in the road. His heart pounded with excitement when he saw that it was a well-filled pocketbook. He was not long in securing it.

Opening the wallet, he found it was absolutely stuffed with bank bills, some of large denominations. There were, besides, several papers to which he paid little attention. They assured him, however, as he had already surmised, that the wallet was the property of Squire Hudson.

"I wonder how much money there is here," thought Tom, with natural curiosity.

He stepped into the woods to avoid notice and carefully counted the bills. There were two hundred-dollar bills, and three fifties, and so many of smaller denominations that Tom found the whole to amount to five hundred and sixty-seven dollars.

"Almost six hundred dollars!" exclaimed Tom, in excitement, for he had never seen so much money before. "How happy should I be if I had as much money! How rich the squire is! He ought to be a happy man."

Then the thought stole into our hero's mind that the wallet contained nearly three times as much as he would need to take him to California.

"If it were only mine!" he thought to himself.

Perhaps Tom ought to have been above temptation, but he was not. For one little instant he was tempted to take out two hundred dollar and then drop the wallet where he had picked it up. No one would probably find out where the missing money was. But Tom had been too well brought up to yield to this temptation. Not even the thought that he might, perhaps within a year, return the money with interest, prevailed upon him.

"It wouldn't be honest," he decided, "and if I began in that way I could not expect that God would prosper me. If that is the only way by which I can go to California, I must make up my mind to stay at home."

So the question was settled in Tom's mind. The money must be returned to the owner.

His pail was nearly full of huckleberries, but he postponed going home, for he felt that Squire Hudson would be feeling anxious about his loss, and he thought it his duty to go and return the money first of all. Accordingly he made his way directly to the imposing residence of the rich man.

Passing up the walk which led to the front door, Tom rang the bell. This was answered by a cross-looking servant. She glanced at the pail of berries and said quickly, "We don't want any berries, and if we did you ought to go round to the side door."

"I haven't asked you to buy any berries, have I?" said Tom, rather provoked by the rudeness of the girl, when he had come to do the squire a favor.

"No, but that's what you're after. We have bought all we want."

"I tell you I didn't come here to sell berries," said Tom independently. "I picked these for use at home."

"Then what do you come here for, anyway, takin' up my time wid comin' to the door, when I'm busy gettin' supper?"

"I want to see Squire Hudson."

"I don't know if he's at home."

"Then you'd better find out and not keep me waiting."

"I never seen such impudence," cried the girl.

"I mean what I say," continued Tom stoutly. "I want to see the squire on important business."

"Much business you have wid him!" said the girl scornfully.

Tom, by this time, was out of patience.

"Go and tell your master that I wish to see him," he said firmly.

"I've a great mind to slam the door in your face," returned Bridget angrily.

"I wouldn't advise you to," said Tom calmly.

A stop was put to the contention by an irritable voice.

"What's all this, hey? Who's at the door, Bridget?"

"A boy wid berries, sir."

"Tell him I don't want any."

"I have told him, and he won't go."

"Won't go, hey?" and Squire Hudson came out into the hall. "What's all this, I say? Won't go?"

"I wish to see you, sir," said Tom, undaunted. "I have told the girl that I didn't come here to sell berries, but she objects to my seeing you."

Squire Hudson was far from an amiable man, and this explanation made him angry with the servant. He turned upon her fiercely.

"What do you mean, you trollop," he demanded, "by refusing to let the boy see me? What do you mean by your insolence, I say?"

Bridget was overwhelmed, for the squire's temper was like a tornado.

"I thought he wanted to sell berries," she faltered.

"That isn't true," said Tom. "I told you expressly that I picked the berries for use at home and had none to sell."

"Go back to the kitchen, you trollop!" thundered the squire. "You deserve to go to jail for your outrageous conduct."

Bridget did not venture to answer a word, for it would only have raised a more violent storm, but instead she retreated crestfallen to her own realm and left our hero in possession of the field. She contented herself with muttering under her breath what she did not dare to speak aloud.

"You are Tom Nelson, are you not?" asked the squire, adjusting his spectacles and looking more carefully at the boy.

"Yes, sir."

"Have you any message from your father?"

"No, sir."

"Then why did you come here to take up my time?" demanded the squire, frowning.

"I came to do you a service, Squire Hudson."

"You came—to—do—me—a—service?" repeated the squire slowly.

"Yes, sir."

"You may as well come in," said the rich man, leading into the sitting room.

Tom followed him into a handsomely furnished room, and the two sat down opposite each other.

CHAPTER III

TOM ASKS FOR A LOAN

"I don't know what service you can do me," said Squire Hudson incredulously. His manner implied, "I am a rich man and you are a poor boy. How can you possibly serve me?"

"Have you lost anything lately?" inquired Tom, coming at once to business.

I suppose most men, when asked such a question, would first think of their wallets. It was so with Squire Hudson. He hastily thrust his hand into his pocket and found a large hole, through which, doubtless, the wallet had slipped.

"I have lost my wallet," he said anxiously. "Have you found it?"

In reply Tom produced the missing article. The squire took it hurriedly, and, at once opening it, counted the money. It was all there, and he heaved a sigh of relief, for he was a man who cared for money more than most people.

"Where did you find it?" he asked.

Tom answered the question.

"It is very fortunate you came along before anyone else saw it. I rode that way on horseback this morning. I told Mrs. Hudson that my pocket needed repairing, but she put it off, according to her usual custom. If it had not been found, I would have kept her on short allowance for a year to come."

Tom felt rather embarrassed, for, of course, it would not do to join in with the squire in his complaints about his wife. Suddenly Squire Hudson asked, eying him keenly, "Do you know how much money there is in this wallet?"

"Yes, sir."

"Then you counted it?"

"Yes, sir."

"Why did you do it?"

"I wanted to know how much there was, so that no one might blame me if any were missing."

"Didn't you want to take any?" asked the squire bluntly.

"Yes," answered Tom promptly.

"Why didn't you? For fear you would be found out?"

"That may have had something to do with it, but it was principally because it would have been stealing and stealing is wrong."

"What would you have done with the money if you had taken it?"

"Started for California next week," answered Tom directly.

"Eh?" cried the squire, rather astonished. "Why do you want to go to California -- a boy like you?"

"To dig gold. I suppose a boy can dig gold as well as a man. There doesn't seem to be much chance for me here. There's nothing to do but to work on the farm, and father and Walter can do all there is to be done there."

"How is your father getting along?" asked the rich man, with an interest which rather surprised Tom.

"Poorly," said Tom. "He makes both ends meet, but we all have to do without a great many things that we need."

The squire looked thoughtful. He took half a dollar from his wallet and tendered it to Tom.

"You've done me a service," he said. "Take that."

Tom drew back.

"I would rather not take money for being honest," he said.

"That's all nonsense," said Squire Hudson sharply.

"That's the way I feel about it," said Tom stoutly.

"Then you're a fool."

"I hope not, sir."

"This would have been quite a large loss to me. I am perfectly willing to give you this money."

Then Tom gathered courage and said boldly, "You can do me a great favor, Squire Hudson, if you choose."

"What is it?"

"Lend me enough money to go to California," said Tom nervously.

"Good gracious! Is the boy crazy?" cried the astonished squire.

"No, sir, I am not crazy. I'll tell you what my plans are. I shall go to work directly when I get there and shall devote the first money I make to paying you. Of course, I shall expect to pay high interest. I am willing to pay you three hundred dollars for two; unless I am sick, I think I can do it inside of twelve months."

"How much money do you suppose you will need for this wild goose expedition?"

"About two hundred dollars, sir, and, as I just said, I will give you my note for three."

"A boy's note is worth nothing."

"Perhaps it isn't in law, but I wouldn't rest till it was paid back."

"What security have you to offer?"

"None, sir, except my word."

"Do you know what I would be if I lent you this money?"

"You would be very kind."

"Pish! I should be a fool."

"I don't think you'd lose anything by it, sir, but, of course, I can't blame you for refusing," and Tom rose to go.

"Sit down again," said the squire. "I want to talk to you about this matter. How long have you been thinking of California?"

"Only two or three days, sir."

"What made you think of it?"

"I wanted to help father."

"Who has told you about California?"

"I have read about it in the papers."

"Have you spoken to your father about going there?"

"I have spoken to him about leaving home and seeking my fortune, but I have not mentioned going to California because I thought it impossible to raise the necessary money."

"Of course. That's sensible, at least."

**An 1849 California Gold Rush flier advertising
steamship transportation**

Squire Hudson rose and walked thoughtfully about the room, occasionally casting a keen glance at Tom, who remained sitting, with his pail of huckleberries in his cap.

After a while the squire spoke again.

"Your father might let you have the money," he suggested.

"My father has no money to spare," said Tom quickly.

"Couldn't he raise some?"

"I don't know how."

"Then I'll tell you. I hold a mortgage for two thousand dollars on his farm. I suppose you know that?"

"Yes, sir."

"I might be willing to increase the mortgage to twenty-two hundred, and he could lend you the extra two hundred."

This was a new idea to Tom, and he took a little time to think it over.

"I don't like to ask father to do that," he said. "He finds it very hard now to pay the interest on the mortgage."

"I thought you intended to pay the money in a year," said the squire sharply.

14

"So I do," said Tom, and he began to think more favorably of the plan.

"In that case your father wouldn't suffer."

"You are right, sir. If father would only consent to do so, I would be happy. But I might die."

"Your father would have to take that risk. You can't expect me to."

This seemed fair enough, and, in fact, the danger didn't seem very great to Tom. He was about sixteen, and to a boy of sixteen death seems very far off, provided he is strong and vigorous, as Tom was. He rapidly decided that the squire's offer was not to be refused without careful consideration. It opened to him a career which looked bright and promising. Once in California, what could he not do? Tom was hopeful and sanguine and did not allow himself to think of failure.

"I understand that you are willing to advance the money, Squire Hudson?" he said, determined to know just what to depend upon.

"I will advance two hundred dollars, on the condition that your father will secure me with an increased mortgage. It is no particular object to me, for I can readily invest the money in some other way."

"I will speak to father about it, Squire Hudson, and meanwhile I am thankful to you for making the offer."

"Very well. Let me know as soon as possible," said the squire carelessly.

As Tom went out, the rich man soliloquized: "I have no faith in the boy's scheme, and I don't believe half the stories they tell about the California mines, but it will give me an extra hold on Nelson and hasten the day when the farm will come into my hands. When Mary Nelson refused my hand I resolved some day to have my revenge. I have waited long, but it will come at last. When she and her children are paupers, she may regret the slight she put upon me."

CHAPTER IV

TOM ASKS FOR A

LEAVE OF ABSENCE

Tom walked home slowly, but the distance seemed short, for he was absorbed in thought. In a way very unexpected he seemed to be likely to realize what he had regarded as a very pleasant, but impossible, dream. Would his father consent to the squire's proposal, and, if so, ought Tom to consent to expose him to the risk of losing so considerable a sum of money? If he had been older and more cautious he would probably have decided in the negative; but Tom was hopeful and sanguine, and the stories he had heard of California had dazzled him. There was, of course, an element of uncertainty in his calculations, but the fact that there seemed to be no prospect before him in his native village had an important influence in shaping his decision.

To ask his father the momentous question, however, was not easy, and he delayed doing it, hoping for a favorable opportunity of introducing the subject. His thoughtful manner excited attention and secured him the opportunity he sought.

"You seem deep in thought, Tom," said his mother.

"Yes, mother, I have a good deal to think about."

"Anybody would think Tom was overwhelmed with business," said Walter, next to Tom in age, with good-humored banter.

"I am," said Tom gravely.

"Won't you take me in partnership, then?" asked Walter.

Tom smiled.

"I don't think I could do that," he answered. "Not to keep you waiting, Squire Hudson has made me a business proposal this afternoon."

All were surprised and looked to Tom for an explanation.

"He offers to advance me two hundred dollars for a year, to help me out to California."

"Squire Hudson makes this offer to a boy of your age?" said his father slowly.

"Yes, or rather he makes the offer to you."

"To me?"

"Perhaps you will think me selfish for even mentioning it," said Tom rapidly, in a hurry to explain fully now that the ice was broken. "He will advance the money, on the condition that you increase the mortgage on the farm to twenty-two hundred dollars."

Mr. Nelson looked blank.

"Do you know, Tom," he said, "how hard I find it now to pay the interest on the mortgage, and how hopeless I am of ever paying it off?"

"I know all that, father, but I want to help you. If I keep my health and have a chance, I think I can help you. There's no chance for me here, and there is a chance in California. You remember what we have read in the Weekly Messenger about the gold fields and what large sums have been realized by miners."

"They are men, and you are a boy."

"That's true," said Tom, "but," he added, with natural pride, "I am pretty strong for a boy. I am willing to work, and I don't see why I can't dig gold as well as a man. I may not make as much, but if I only do half as well as some that we have read about, I can do a good deal for you."

"How far off is California?" asked Mrs. Nelson.

"Over three thousand miles, across the continent," answered her husband. "By sea it is a good deal more."

"Why, it is as far off as Europe," said Walter, who was fresh from his lesson in geography.

"It is farther than some parts of Europe -- England, for example," said his father.

"And a wild, unsettled region," said Mrs. Nelson soberly.

This 1852 map depicts the height of the Gold Rush in the United States.

"I don't think so much of that," said Mark Nelson. "Tom is no baby. He is a boy of good sense, not heedless, like some of his age, and I should feel considerable confidence in his getting along well."

"What, Mark, are you in favor of his going so far -- a boy who has never been away from home in his life?"

"I don't know what to say. I have not had time to consider the matter, as it has come upon me suddenly. I have a good deal of confidence in Tom, but there is one difficulty in my mind."

"What is that, father?" asked Tom anxiously.

"The expense of getting to California, and the method of raising the money; I don't like to increase the mortgage."

"I suppose you are right, father," said Tom slowly. "I know it is more than I have any right to ask. I wouldn't even have mentioned it if I hadn't hoped to help you to pay it back."

"That is understood, Tom," said his father kindly. "I know you mean what you say, and that you would redeem your promise if fortune, or rather Providence, permitted. It is a serious matter, however, and not to be decided in a hurry. We will speak of it again."

Nothing more was said about Tom's plan till after the children had gone to bed. Then, as Mark Nelson and his wife sat before the fire in the open fireplace, the subject was taken up anew.

"Mary," said Mark, "I am beginning to think favorably of Tom's proposal."

"How can you say so, Mark?" interrupted his wife. "It seems like madness to send a young boy so far away."

"Tom can't be called a young boy; he is now sixteen."

"But he has never been away from home."

"He must go some time."

"If it were only to Boston or New York ... but to go more than three thousand miles away!" and the mother shuddered.

"There are dangers as great in Boston or New York as in California, Mary, to a boy of Tom's age. He can't always be surrounded by home influences."

"I wish we could find employment for him in town," said Mrs. Nelson uneasily.

"That is a mother's thought, and it would be pleasant for all of us, but I doubt if it would be better for Tom."

"Why not?"

"A boy who is thrown upon his own guardianship and his own resources develops manliness and self-reliance sooner than at home. But we need not take that into consideration; there is nothing to do here, nor is there likely to be. He must go away from home to find employment. To obtain a job in Boston or New York requires influence and friends in those places, and we can hope for neither. In California he will become his own employer. The gold-mines are open to all, and he may earn in a year as much as he could in five years in the East."

"Do you favor his going, then, Mark?"

"Not against your will, Mary. Indeed, I should not feel justified in increasing the mortgage upon our little property against your wish. That concerns us all."

"I don't think so much of that. I am so afraid Tom would get sick in California. What would become of the poor boy in that case?"

"That is a mother's thought. I think Tom would find friends who would not let him suffer. He is a manly, attractive boy, though he is ours, and I think he is well calculated to make his way."

"That he is," said his mother proudly. "No one can help liking Tom."

"Then you see he is likely to find friends. Were he such a boy as Sinclair Hudson, I should feel afraid that he would fare badly, if he stood in need of help from others. Sinclair is certainly a very disagreeable boy."

"Yes, he is, and he isn't half as smart as Tom."

"A mother's vanity," said Mark Nelson, smiling. "However, you are right there. I should consider it a misfortune to have such a cross-grained, selfish son as Sinclair. Squire Hudson, with all his wealth, is not fortunate in his only child. There is considerable resemblance between father and son. I often wish that someone other than the squire held the mortgage on our farm."

"You don't think he would take advantage of you?"

"I don't think he would be very lenient on me if I failed to pay interest promptly. He has a grudge against me, you know."

"That is nonsense," said Mrs. Nelson, blushing, for she understood the allusion.

"I am glad he doesn't ask me to give him a mortgage on you, Mary."

"He has forgotten all that," said Mrs. Nelson. "I am no longer young and pretty."

"I think you more attractive than ever," said the husband.

"Because you are foolish," said his wife, but she was well pleased, nevertheless. Poor as her husband was, she had never dreamed of regretting her choice.

"Be it so, but about this affair of Tom -- what shall I say to him in the morning?"

Mrs. Nelson recovered her gravity instantly.

"Decide as you think right, Mark," she said. "If you judge that Tom had better go I will do my best to become reconciled to his absence and set about getting him ready."

"It is a great responsibility, Mary," said Mark slowly, "but I accept it. Let the boy go, if he wishes. He will leave our care, but we can trust him to the care of his heavenly Father, who will be as near to him in California as at home."

Thus Tom's future was decided. His father and mother retired to bed but not to sleep. They were parting already in imagination with their first-born, and the thought of that parting was sad indeed.

CHAPTER V

TOM RAISES THE MONEY

Tom got up early the next morning -- in fact, he was up first in the house -- and attended to his usual "chores." He was splitting wood when his father passed him on the way to the barn with the milk pail in his hand.

"You are up early, Tom," he said.

"Yes," answered our hero.

Tom could not help wondering whether his father had come to any decision about letting him go to California, but he did not like to ask. In due time he would learn, of course. He felt that he should like to have it decided one way or the other. While his plans were in doubt he felt unsettled and nervous.

At an early hour the family gathered about the breakfast table. Tom noticed that his father and mother looked grave and spoke in a subdued tone, as if they had something on their minds, but he did not know what to infer from this, except that they had his prospects still in consideration.

When breakfast was over, Mark Nelson pushed back his chair and said, "How soon can you get Tom ready to start, Mary?"

"Am I going, father?" asked Tom, his heart giving an eager bound.

"Is Tom really going?" asked the younger children, with scarcely less eagerness.

"If Squire Hudson doesn't go back on his promise. Tom, you can go with me to the squire's."

"How soon?"

"In about an hour. He doesn't eat breakfast as early as we do. I think he will be ready to receive us in about an hour."

"Thank you, father," said Tom. "You are doing a great deal for me."

"I can't do much for you, my boy. I can probably get you to California, and then you will be thrown upon your own exertions."

"I mean to work very hard. I think I shall succeed."

"I hope so at least, Tom. When the time comes for the other boys to start working, I shall be glad to have your help in doing it."

Tom was pleased to hear this, though it placed upon his shoulders a new and heavy responsibility. He was assuming the responsibility not only for his own future but for that of his brothers. But it made him feel more grown up, as if the period of his dependent boyhood were over, and he had become a young man all at once.

"I hope I sha'n't disappoint you, father," he said.

"If you do, I don't think it will be your fault, Tom," said his father kindly. "Fortune may be against you, but we must take that risk."

"I don't know what to think about it, Tom," said his mother, in a tone of doubt and mental disturbance. "I feel as if you were too young to go out in the wide world to seek your fortune."

"I am not so very young, mother. I am old enough to make my way."

"So your father says, and I have yielded to his judgment, but, Tom, I don't know how to let you go."

There were tears in Mrs. Nelson's eyes as she spoke. Tom was moved, and if he needed anything to strengthen him in the good resolutions he had formed, his mother's emotion supplied it.

"You sha'n't regret giving your consent, mother," he said manfully, and, rising from his seat, he went to his mother and kissed her.

"Mary," said Mr. Nelson, "you haven't answered my question. How long will it take to get Tom ready? If he is to go, he may as well start as soon as possible."

"Let me see," said Mrs. Nelson, "how many shirts have you got, Tom?"

"Five."

"Are they all in good order?"

"I believe one needs mending."

"I don't know whether that will be enough," said Mrs. Nelson doubtfully.

"Mary," said her husband, "don't provide too large a supply of clothing. Tom may find it a burden. Remember, in California, he will have to travel on foot and carry his own baggage."

"Then I think he is already pretty well provided. But some of his clothes may need mending. That won't take long, and I will attend to it at once."

"Perhaps Squire Hudson will go back on his word, after all," said Walter.

—

Tom's face was overcast. That would be a disappointment he could not easily bear.

"I shall soon know," he said.

An hour later Tom and his father set out for Squire Hudson's residence. Tom felt nervous; he could not well help it.

"Tom," said his father, "this is an important visit for you."

"Yes, sir," said Tom.

"You are feeling nervous, I see. Try to take it coolly and don't feel too low-spirited if things don't turn out as you hope."

"I will try to follow your advice, father, but I am not sure that I can."

"If you are disappointed, try to think it is for the best. A boy of your age had made all arrangements to visit Europe with a party of friends. The day before starting something happened which made it impossible for him to go. For weeks he had been looking forward with eager anticipation to his journey, and now it was indefinitely postponed."

"What a terrible disappointment!" said Tom.

"Yes, it seemed so, but mark the issue. The steamer was lost, and all on board were drowned. The disappointment saved his life."

"It might not always turn out so," objected Tom.

"No, that is true. Still, if we are willing to think that our disappointments are not always misfortunes, we shall go through life with more cheerfulness and content."

"Still, I hope I shall not be disappointed in this," said Tom.

"You are perhaps too young to be philosophical," said his father.

Mark Nelson had enjoyed only the usual advantages of education afforded by a common school, but he was a man of good natural capacity and more thoughtful than many in his vocation. From him Tom inherited good natural abilities and industrious habits. It would not be fair, however, to give all the credit to his father. Mrs. Nelson was a superior woman, and all her children were well endowed by nature.

As they turned into Squire Hudson's gravel path, the squire himself opened the front door.

"Were you coming to see me?" he asked.

"We would like to speak with you a few minutes, squire, if you can spare the time."

"Oh, yes, I have nothing pressing on hand," said the squire, with unusual affability. "Walk in, Mr. Nelson."

He led the way into the room where Tom had had his interview with him the day before.

"Your son did me a good turn yesterday," he said graciously. "He behaved in a very creditable manner."

"He told me that he found your wallet, Squire Hudson."

"Yes. It contained a large sum of money. Some boys would have kept it."

"None of my boys would," said Mark Nelson proudly.

"Of course not. They're too well brought up."

"Tom told me that you offered to advance money enough to get him to California," said Mr. Nelson, coming to business.

"On satisfactory security," added the squire cautiously.

"You proposed to increase the mortgage on my place?"

"Yes," said the squire. "I wouldn't have done it, though, Neighbor Nelson, but for the good turn the boy did me. I am not at all particular about increasing the amount of the mortgage, but, if by so doing it I can promote Tom's views, I won't object."

"Thank you, sir," said Tom gratefully.

"It is a serious step for me to take," continued Mr. Nelson, "for I feel the encumbrance to be a heavy one already. In fact, it is with difficulty that I pay the interest. But the time has come when Tom should start in life, and in this village there seems to be no opening."

"None whatever," said the squire, in a tone of decision.

"What do you think of the prospects in California?" asked Mark Nelson. "You are a man of business and can judge better than I. Are the stories we hear of fortunes made in a short time to be relied upon?"

"As to that," said the squire deliberately, "I suppose we can't believe all we hear; we must make some allowances. But, after all, there's no doubt of the existence of gold in large quantities; I am sure of that."

"Then about the wisdom of sending out a boy like Tom, alone: do you think it best?"

"It depends altogether on the boy," responded the squire. "If he is honest, industrious, and energetic, he will make his way. You know your own boy better than I do."

"He is all you say, Squire Hudson. I have a great deal of confidence in Tom."

Tom looked at his father gratefully. Sometimes it does a boy good to learn that the older people have confidence in him.

"Then let him go," said the squire. "I stand ready to furnish the money. I think you said you needed two hundred dollars."

This question was put to Tom, and the boy answered in the affirmative.

"Very well," said the squire. "As soon as the necessary writings are made out, the money shall be ready."

"It's all settled!" thought Tom triumphantly.

At that moment Sinclair Hudson, the squire's only son, opened the door and looked into the room.

"Hello, Tom Nelson," said he rather rudely. "What brings you here?"

CHAPTER VI

TOM ARRIVES IN PITTSBURGH

"I came on business, Sinclair," answered Tom, smiling.

"Thomas is going to California, Sinclair," explained Squire Hudson.

Sinclair opened wide his eyes in amazement. "What for?" he asked.

"To dig gold and make my fortune," answered Tom complacently.

"Come out and tell me all about it."

"You can go, Thomas," said Squire Hudson graciously. "Your father and I will settle the business."

"Is it true that you are going to California?" asked Sinclair, when they were out in the front yard.

"Yes."

"How soon do you go?"

"I want to get away in a week."

"What has my father to do with it?" inquired Sinclair.

"He is going to lend me the money to get there."

"How much?"

"Two hundred dollars."

"Then he is a greater fool than I thought," said Sinclair, with characteristic politeness.

"Why do you say that?" demanded our hero, justly nettled.

"Because he'll never see the money again."

"Yes, he will. My father is responsible for it."

"Your father is a poor man."

"He is able to pay that, if I don't, but I hope he won't have to."

"Do you really expect to find gold?" asked Sinclair curiously.

"Certainly I do. Others have, and why shouldn't I? I am willing to work hard."

"Do you think you'll come home rich?"

"I hope so."

"I have a great mind to ask father to let me go with you," said Sinclair unexpectedly.

"You wouldn't like it. You haven't been brought up to work," said Tom, rather startled, and not much pleased with the proposal, for Sinclair Hudson was about the last boy he wished as a companion.

"Oh, I wouldn't go to work. I would go as a gentleman, to see the country. Wait a minute; I will run in and ask him."

So Sinclair ran into the house and made his request.

"That's a wild idea, Sinclair," said his father quickly.

"Why is it? I'm as old as Tom Nelson."

"He is going because it is necessary for him to earn his living."

"He will have a splendid time," grumbled the spoiled son.

"You shall travel all you want when you are older," said his father. "Now you must get an education."

"I want to travel now."

"I will take you to New York the next time I go."

"Give me five dollars besides."

The money was handed to him.

He went out and reported to Tom that he was going to travel all over the world when he was a little older and had decided not to go to California now.

"If you have money enough you can go with me," he added graciously.

"Thank you," said Tom politely, though the prospect of having Sinclair for a traveling companion did not exhilarate him much.

For a few days Mrs. Nelson was very busy getting Tom ready to go. It was well, perhaps, that so much needed to be done, for it kept her mind from the thought of the separation.

The question of which route to take, whether by steamer or across the plains, demanded consideration. It was finally decided that Tom should go overland. It was thought he might join some company at St. Joseph -- or St. Joe, as it was then, and is now, popularly called -- and pay his passage in services, thus saving a good share of the two hundred dollars. That was, of course, an important consideration.

"How shall I carry my money?" asked Tom.

"It will be best to take gold and carry it for safety in a belt around your waist," said his father. "You must be very prudent and careful, or you may be robbed. That would be a serious thing for you, as I could not forward you any more money."

"I will be very prudent, father," said Tom. "I know the value of money too well to risk losing it."

Well, the days of preparation were over at length, and Tom stood on the threshold, bidding goodbye to his parents and his brothers and sisters. He had not realized till now what it was to leave home on a long journey of indefinite duration. He wanted to be heroic, but in spite of himself his eyes moistened, and he came near breaking down.

"I don't know how to part with you, my dear child," said his mother.

Think that it is all for the best, mother," said Tom, choking. "Think of the time when I will come back with plenty of money."

"God bless you, Tom!" said his father. "Don't forget your good habits and principles when you are far away from us."

"I won't, father."

**Tom's family gathers at their humble farmhouse
to say goodbye to Tom.**

So Tom's long journey commenced.

Tom's plan was to go to St. Louis first. His father made some inquiries about the route and recommended going to Pittsburgh by train, then to take the boat on the Ohio River for Cincinnati. This seemed to Tom to afford a pleasant variety, and he gladly accepted the suggestion.

As they were approaching Pittsburgh, Tom occupied a whole seat on the left-hand side of the car. A brisk, plausible young man of twenty-five, passing through the aisle, observed the vacant seat and, pausing, inquired, "Is this seat engaged?"

"No, sir," answered Tom.

"Then, if you have no objection, I will occupy it."

"Certainly, sir."

The young man was nicely dressed. In his bosom sparkled a diamond pin, and he wore three or four rings on his fingers.

"He must be rich," thought Tom, who was of an observant turn.

"A pleasant day to travel," remarked the young man affably.

"Yes, it is," said Tom.

"Do you go farther than Pittsburgh?"

"Yes, I am going to California," answered Tom proudly.

"Is it possible? Are you alone?"

"Yes, sir."

"You are young to travel so far."

"I am sixteen -- that is, I shall be in two or three weeks."

"Still, you are young to take such a journey alone. Are you going to join friends there?"

"No, I am going to seek my fortune."

Once more the young man looked surprised and scanned Tom curiously.

"I presume you are from the city," he observed, with a smile which Tom would not have understood if he had noticed it. The truth is that Tom bore evident marks of being a country boy. I don't like to say that he looked "green," but he certainly lacked the air that distinguishes a town-bred boy. His companion evidently understood boy nature, for Tom was much flattered by the supposition that he was a city boy.

"No," he answered, almost as if apologizing for a discreditable fact. "I am from the country."

"You don't say so!" exclaimed the other, in apparent surprise. "I thought, from your appearance, that you were from the city. How do you go from Pittsburgh?"

"By river to Cincinnati."

"Do you really? I am glad to hear it; I am going there myself. We shall be fellow passengers. That will be pleasant."

Tom thought it would. His companion seemed very pleasant and social, and he had been feeling lonely, as was only natural.

"Yes, it will," he said.

"By the way, as we may be thrown together, more or less, we ought to know each other. My name is Milton Graham. My father is a rich merchant in New York. I am traveling partly on business for my father's firm and partly for pleasure."

"My name is Thomas Nelson; most people call me Tom," said our hero.

"Then I will call you Tom," said Graham. "I like the name. I have a favorite cousin named Tom. Poor boy!—he is an orphan. His father died two years ago, leaving him two hundred thousand dollars. My father is his guardian. He is about your age, only not quite so good-looking."

Tom blushed. He had not thought much of his own looks, but he was human, and no one is displeased at being considered good-looking. Mr. Graham spoke meditatively, as if he was not intending to pay a compliment, only mentioning a fact, and Tom did not feel called upon to thank him for this flattering remark.

"That is a great deal of money," he said.

"Yes, it is. All my relations are rich, that is, except one uncle, who probably is not worth over twenty thousand dollars."

Tom was impressed. A man who could talk of such a sum in such terms must certainly be very rich.

"Do you know, Mr. Graham," he inquired, "how soon the steamer will start after we reach Pittsburgh?"

"No, but I can find out after we reach there."

On arriving at Pittsburgh, inquiry was made, and it was ascertained that the steamer River Belle would leave at nine o'clock the following morning.

"We shall have to go to a hotel," said Graham.

"Is there any cheap hotel here?" asked Tom prudently.

"Yes, there is the Pittsburgh House. Suppose we both go there."

"All right."

Mr. Graham had only a small carpetbag, smaller than Tom's. They took them in their hands and walked for a short distance, till they reached a plain building, which, from the sign, Tom discovered to be the hotel which had been mentioned.

"Shall we room together? It will cost less," said Milton Graham carelessly.

"If you please," said Tom.

He was lonely and thought he would like company. Besides, it would be cheaper, and that was a weighty consideration.

CHAPTER VII

THE PITTSBURGH HOUSE

Tom and his companion entered the hotel. At the left was the clerk's desk. Milton Graham naturally took the lead. He took a pen from the clerk and entered his name with a flourish. Then he handed the pen to Tom, who followed his example, omitting the flourish, however.

"This young gentleman will room with me," said Graham.

"All right, sir," said the clerk. "Will you go up to your room now?"

"Yes."

The porter was summoned and handed the key of No. 16. He took the two carpetbags and led the way upstairs, for the Pittsburgh House had no elevator. Even in the best hotels at that time this modern convenience was not to be found.

The door of No. 16 was opened, revealing a plain room, about twelve feet square, provided, as Tom was glad to see, with two narrow beds.

"Have you got a quarter, Tom?" asked Graham.

Tom drew one from his pocket.

Graham took it and handed it to the porter, who expressed his thanks.

"It's always customary to tip the porter," he said carelessly, in answer to Tom's look of surprise.

"What for?"

"For bringing up the baggage."

"Twenty-five cents for bringing up two small carpetbags! That's pretty high. I'd have brought them up myself, if I had known," said Tom, dissatisfied, for he felt that this fee was hardly in accordance with his resolutions of economy.

"Oh, he expects it. It's his regular perquisite. When you've traveled more you'll understand."

"How much are we to pay for our accommodations?" asked Tom anxiously.

"About two dollars apiece, I reckon."

"That's more than I can afford," said Tom, alarmed.

"Perhaps it is less, as we room together."

"I hope so, for I can't afford to be extravagant."

"Do you call two dollars a day extravagant?" asked Graham, smiling.

"It is for me. My father is poor."

"Oh, it'll be all right. I'll fix it with the clerk. If you are ready, suppose we go down and have some supper."

To this Tom had no objection. He washed his hands and face and brushed his hair; then he declared himself ready.

Tom was hungry and did justice to the supper, which he found very good. As they left the table, and re-entered the office of the hotel, Milton Graham said, "I am going to make a call on some friends. Sorry to leave you, but we shall meet later in the evening."

"All right," said Tom.

On the whole he did not regret being alone. He began to doubt whether Graham would make a desirable traveling companion. Tom felt the need of economy, and he saw that his companion would make it difficult. If a fee must be paid, it was fair to divide it, but the porter's fee had come out of Tom's pocket.

"Didn't he have a quarter, I wonder?" thought our hero.

It was a small matter, but economy must begin in small matters, or it is not likely to be practiced at all.

He took the opportunity to go to the desk and ascertain the sum likely to be charged for his accommodations.

"How long do you stay?" asked the clerk pleasantly.

"Till tomorrow morning. I am going to sail in the River Belle."

"Then we shall charge you a dollar and a half."

This seemed large to Tom, but he made no objection.

"How much would it have been if I had roomed alone?" he asked.

"The same. We make no change in our terms on that account."

"Mr. Graham told me it would be cheaper to room together."

"He is your roommate, isn't he?"

"Yes, sir."

"He is mistaken, so far as our house is concerned. I suppose you have known him for some time."

"No, sir. I met him on the train yesterday afternoon for the first time."

"Then you don't know anything about him?"

"Oh, yes," answered Tom. "He is the son of a rich merchant in New York."

"Who told you that?"

"He did."

The clerk was a man of middle age. At home he had a son of Tom's age, and this led him to feel a friendly interest in our hero.

"I suppose you have never traveled much," he said.

"No, sir. This is my first journey."

"Are you going far?"

"To California."

"That is a long journey for a boy of your age," said the clerk, looking surprised.

"Yes, sir, but I can't find any work to do at home, and I am going to California to seek my fortune."

"I hope you will be successful," said the clerk, with hearty sympathy. "Will you let me give you a piece of advice?"

"I shall be very glad of it, sir," responded Tom. "I find I am quite inexperienced."

"Then don't trust strangers too readily. It is dangerous."

"Do you refer to Mr. Graham?" asked Tom, startled.

"Yes, I refer to him, or any other chance acquaintance."

"Don't you think he is all right?" asked our hero anxiously.

"I don't think he is the son of a rich merchant in New York."

"Then why should he tell me so?"

Tom was green, and I have no intention of concealing it.

"I can't tell what his designs may be. Did you tell him that you were going to California?"

"Yes, sir."

"Then he will, of course, conclude that you have money. Did you tell him where you keep it?"

"No, sir. I keep it in a belt around my waist."

"You are too ready to tell that, though with me the information is safe. You are to room together. What will be easier, then, for your companion to rob you during the night?"

"I'd better take a room alone," said Tom, now thoroughly alarmed.

"I should advise you to, in most cases, but at present it may be as well to let things remain as they are, as it will save an awkward explanation."

"But I don't want to be robbed."

"We have a safe in the office -- there it is -- in which we deposit articles of value entrusted to us by our guests. Then we become responsible for them. I advise you to leave your money with us overnight."

"I will," said Tom, relieved. "I shall have to go to my room to get it."

"Very well. If you have a watch, or any other valuable, it will be well to put those in our charge also."

"No, sir, I have nothing of consequence but the money."

The belt of money was deposited in the safe, and Tom felt relieved. He began to realize for the first time the need for prudence and caution. It had never occurred to him that a nice, gentlemanly-looking man like Milton Graham was likely to rob him of his scanty means. Even now he thought there must be some mistake. Still he felt that he had done the right thing in depositing the money with the clerk. The mere thought of losing it, and finding himself high and dry -- stranded, so to speak -- hundreds of miles from home, made him shudder. On the whole, Tom had learned a valuable, though unpleasant, lesson. The young are by nature trustful. They are disposed to put confidence in those whom they meet, even for the first time. Unhappily, in a world where there is so much evil as there is in ours, such confidence is not justified. There are too many who make it a business to prey on their fellows and select in preference the young and inexperienced.

It was only seven o'clock. Tom had a curiosity to see the city of Pittsburgh, with whose name he had been familiar. So, after parting with his treasure, he went out for a walk. He did not much care where he went, since all was new to him. He ascertained, on inquiry, that Smithfield Street was the principal business thoroughfare. He inquired his way thither and walked slowly through it, his attention fully occupied by what he saw.

CHAPTER VIII

GRAHAM IN HIS TRUE COLORS

Tom strayed into a street leading from the main thoroughfare. Presently he came to a brilliantly-lighted liquor saloon. As he paused in front of the door, a heavy hand was laid upon his shoulder, and, looking up, he met the glance of a well-dressed gentleman, rather portly, whose flushed face and uncertain gait indicated his condition. He leaned rather heavily upon Tom, apparently for support, for he seemed to have been drinking more than was good for him.

"My young friend," he said, "come in and take a drink."

"Thank you, sir, but I would rather not," said Tom, startled.

"It won't hurt you. It don't hurt me."

As he uttered these last words he came near falling. In his effort to save himself he clutched Tom by the arm and nearly pulled him over. Our hero was anxious to get away.

"Are you sure it don't hurt you?" he could not help saying.

"Do you think I'm drunk?" demanded the other.

"I think you've taken more than is good for you, sir," Tom answered bravely.

"I guess you're right," muttered the gentleman, trying to stand upright. "The drink's gone to my legs. That's strange. Does it ever go to your legs?"

"I never drink, sir."

"You're a most extraor'nary young man," hiccoughed Tom's new acquaintance.

"I must bid you good night, sir," said our hero, anxious to get away.

"Don't go. I can't get home alone."

"Where do you live, sir?"

"I live in the country."

"Are you staying at a hotel?"

"Yes -- Pittsburgh House. Know Pittsburgh House?"

"Yes, sir. I am staying there myself. Shall I lead you there? You'd better not drink any more."

"Jus' you say, my young frien'. You know best."

It was not a pleasant, or, indeed, an easy task to lead home the inebriate, for he leaned heavily on Tom, and, being a large man, it was as much as our hero could do to get him along. As they were walking along Tom caught sight of his roommate, Milton Graham, just turning into a saloon, in company with two other young men. They were laughing loudly and seemed in high spirits. Graham did not recognize Tom.

"I hope he won't come home drunk," thought our hero. "It seems to me it is fashionable to drink here."

Tom's experience of city life was very limited. It was not long before he learned that Pittsburgh was by no means exceptional in this respect.

He ushered his companion safely into the hotel, and then a servant took charge of him and led him to his room. Tom sat up a little while longer, reading a paper he found in the office, and then went to bed.

"I suppose Mr. Graham will come home late," he said to himself. "I must leave the door unlocked."

He soon went to sleep. How long he slept he did not know, but he suddenly awoke after an interval. Opening his eyes he became conscious that Graham had returned. He discovered something more. His roommate, partially undressed, and with his back turned to Tom, was engaged in searching our hero's pockets. This discovery set Tom broad awake at once. He was not frightened, but rather amused when he thought of Graham's disappointment. He did not think it best to speak but counterfeited sleep.

"I wonder where the boy keeps his money," he heard Graham mutter. "Perhaps it is in his coat pocket. No, there is nothing but a handkerchief. He's more careful than I gave him credit for. Perhaps it is under his pillow."

He laid down the clothes and approached the bed. Tom, with some effort, kept his eyes firmly closed.

Graham slid his hand lightly under the pillow but withdrew it with all exclamation of disappointment.

"He must have some money," he muttered. "Ah, I have it! It is in his valise."

He approached Tom's valise, but it was locked. He drew out a bunch of keys and tried one after the other, but it was in vain. Our hero feared he might resort to violent means of opening it, and he turned in bed. Graham wheeled round quickly.

Tom stretched and opened his eyes languidly.

"Is that you, Mr. Graham?" he asked.

"Yes," answered Graham nonchalantly, proceeding to undress himself. "Have you been abed long?"

"I don't know," answered Tom. "What time is it?"

"Haven't you got a watch?"

"No, I am not rich enough."

"It is one o'clock. I hadn't seen my friend for a long time and couldn't get away till late. By the way, have you got a key about you? I can't open my carpetbag."

Tom thought of suggesting the bunch of keys in Graham's pocket but decided not to.

"My key is in my pants' pocket."

"Suppose you get it," said Graham. "I don't like to feel in another person's pocket. There might be some money there."

This was very scrupulous for one who had already searched all Tom's pockets thoroughly.

Our hero got up, and got the key for his roommate.

"No, it won't fit," said the young man, after a brief trial. "It is too large."

Tom replaced the key in his pocket, confident that Graham would in the course of the night use it to open his valise. This, however, did not trouble him.

"He won't think it worth while to steal my shirts or stockings," he reflected, "and the handkerchiefs are not worth taking."

"It will be rather awkward if I can't find my keys," said Graham craftily. "I keep my money in my valise."

He thought his unsophisticated companion would reveal in turn where he kept his money, but Tom only said, "That is a good place," and, turning over, closed his eyes again.

During the night Tom's valise was opened, as he ascertained in a simple way. In the morning he found that the key was in the right hand-pocket instead of the left, in which he had placed it.

Upon Graham's last failure he began to suspect what Tom had done with his money.

"The boy isn't so green as I thought," he said to himself. "Curse his prudence! I must get the money somehow, for I am precious hard up."

He got up early, when Tom was yet asleep, and went down to the office.

"Good morning," he said to the clerk affably.

"Good morning, sir."

"My young friend and roommate left his money with you last night. Please deliver it to me."

"What is the number of your room?" asked the clerk quietly.

"No. 16. Tom Nelson is my roommate."

"Why doesn't he come for it himself?" inquired the hotel clerk, with a searching glance at Graham.

"He wishes me to buy his steamboat ticket," answered Graham coolly. "He is going down the river in my charge."

"Are you his guardian?"

"Yes," answered Graham, with cool effrontery. "He is the son of an acquaintance of mine, and I naturally feel an interest in the boy."

"He told me he never met you till yesterday."

Graham was rather taken aback, but he recovered himself quickly.

"That's pretty cool in Tom," he returned, shrugging his shoulders. "I understand it, though."

"I am glad you do," said the clerk sarcastically, "for it doesn't look to me at all consistent with what you represent."

"The fact is," said Graham plausibly, "Tom has a feeling of independence and doesn't like to have it supposed that he is under anybody's protection. That accounts for what he told you. It isn't right, though, to misrepresent. I must give him a scolding. I am in a little of a hurry, so if you will kindly give me the boy's money -- "

"It won't do, Mr. Graham," said the clerk very firmly. "The money was put in our charge by the boy, and it will be delivered only to him."

"You seem to be very suspicious," said Graham loftily. "Hand me my bill, if you please. I will breakfast elsewhere."

The bill was made out and paid. Five minutes later Milton Graham, with an air of outraged virtue, stalked out of the hotel, quite forgetting the young friend who was under his charge.

When Tom came downstairs he was told of the attempt to get possession of his money.

"I am much obliged to you for not letting him have it," he said. "He searched my clothes and valise during the night, but I said nothing, for I knew he would find nothing worth taking."

"He is a dangerous companion. If you ever meet him again, I advise you to give him a wide berth."

"I certainly shall follow your advice. If you had not warned me against him he would have stolen my money during the night."

CHAPTER IX

THE "RIVER BELLE"

As Tom took his place at the breakfast table, he mechanically lifted his eyes and glanced at his neighbors. Directly opposite him sat the gentleman whom he had brought home the evening before. Now he looked sober and respectable. Indeed, he looked as if he might be a person of some prominence. He met Tom's glance and recognized him.

"I think you are the boy who came home with me last evening," he said.

"Yes, sir," answered Tom, rather embarrassed.

"I am afraid I was not quite myself," continued the stout gentleman.

"Not quite, sir."

"I ought to be ashamed of myself, and I am. I don't often allow myself to be caught in that way. You did me a good service."

"You are quite welcome, sir."

"I had a good deal of money with me, and, if I had drank any more, I should probably have been robbed."

"Why did you run such a risk, sir?" Tom could not help asking.

"Because I was a fool," said the other bluntly. "I have taste for drink, but when I am at home I keep it under control."

"Then you don't live in Pittsburgh, sir?"

"No. My home is in one of the river towns in Ohio. I came to Pittsburgh to collect money due to me for produce, and but for you I should probably have carried none of it home."

"I am very glad to be of service to you," said our hero sincerely.

"What are your plans, my young friend? I suppose you are only a visitor in this city."

"I am on my way to California. I expect to sail in the River Belle at nine o'clock."

"Then we shall be fellow passengers, and I shall have a chance to become better acquainted with you. You are young to go to California alone. You are alone -- are you not?"

"Yes, sir."

They went down to the boat together, and on the way Tom told his story. He learned that his acquaintance was Mr. Nicholas Waterbury, that he had been a member of the Ohio Legislature, and, as he inferred, that he was a prominent citizen of the town in which he lived.

"I should be very much ashamed to have them hear at home how I had forgotten myself," said Mr. Waterbury.

"It need not be known," said Tom. "I shall not mention it to any one."

"Thank you," said Mr. Waterbury. "I would rather you did not, as the news might reach my home."

"Where do you live, sir?"

"In Marietta. I shall be glad to have you leave the boat there and stay a day or two with me."

"Thank you, sir, but I am in a hurry to reach California, on my father's account. I want to send back as soon as possible the money he raised to pay my expenses out."

"That is very commendable; I can enter into your feelings. I should like to show my obligation to you in some way."

"It is not worth thinking about, sir," said Tom modestly.

"Permit me to disagree with you. Why, my young friend, how much money do you think I had with me?"

"I don't know, sir."

"Upward of six hundred dollars."

As Mr. Waterbury uttered these words, a young man, very dark, with narrow black whiskers, passed them. He darted a quick glance at the speaker and walked rapidly on. Tom noticed him but not with attention.

"That is a good deal of money, sir," he remarked.

"It would have been a good deal to lose," said Mr. Waterbury, "and I have no doubt I should have lost it if it had not been for you."

"I haven't so much money as you, but I came near losing it last night."

"How was that?" asked Tom's new acquaintance, with curiosity.

Tom explained the attempt of his roommate to rob him.

"It would have been a serious loss to you, my young friend."

"It would have broken up all my plans, and I should have had to work my way home, greatly disappointed."

You will need to be careful about forming acquaintances. There are exceptions, however. I am a new acquaintance, but I don't think you need fear me."

"No, sir," said Tom, smiling.

"While I have received a great service from you, who are a new acquaintance. But here we are at the steamer."

The River Belle lay at her pier. Tom and his companion went on board. Both secured tickets, and Tom provided himself with a stateroom, for he expected to remain on board till they reached Cincinnati. Freight of various kinds was being busily stowed away below. It was a busy and animated scene, and Tom looked on with interest.

"Have you ever been on a steamboat before?" asked Mr. Waterbury.

"No, sir. I have never traveled anywhere to speak of before leaving home on this journey," replied Tom.

"It will be a pleasant variety for you, then, though the scenery is tame. However, some of the river towns are pretty."

"I am sure I shall like it, sir."

"I wish I were going all the way with you -- I mean as far as Cincinnati," said Mr. Waterbury.

"I wish you were, sir."

"I have a great mind to do it," said the gentleman musingly. "I should have to go very soon on business, at any rate, and I can attend to it now just as well as later."

"I shall be very glad if you can make it convenient, sir. We might occupy the same stateroom."

"Are you not afraid that I shall follow the example of your Pittsburgh roommate?" asked Mr. Waterbury.

"I have less to lose than you," answered Tom. "Besides, I shall have to have a roommate, as there are two berths."

"Precisely, and I might be safer than some. I have a great mind to keep on. I shall see someone on the pier in Marietta by whom I can send word to my family. By the way, I have a son about your age and a daughter two years younger."

"Have you, sir?" asked Tom, with interest.

"I should like you to meet them. Perhaps you may some day."

"I hope I may," said Tom politely.

"I am a manufacturer," continued Mr. Waterbury, "and sell my goods chiefly in Pittsburgh and Cincinnati. From these places they are forwarded farther east and west."

"I suppose that's a pretty good business, sir?"

"Sometimes, but there are intervals of depression. However, I have no right to complain. I began a poor boy, and now I am moderately rich."

"Were you as poor as I am?" inquired Tom, beginning to feel a personal interest in his companion's career.

"Quite so, I fancy. At the age of sixteen I couldn't call myself the owner of five dollars."

"And you have become rich?" said Tom, feeling very much encouraged.

"Moderately so. I am probably worth fifty thousand dollars and am just fifty years of age."

"That seems to me very rich," said Tom.

"I should have said the same thing at your age. Our views change as we get older. Still, I regard myself as very well off, and, with prudent management, I need not fear reverses."

"I should think not," said Tom.

"You don't know how easy it is to lose money, my boy. I am not referring to robbery, but to mismanagement."

"Your success encourages me, Mr. Waterbury," said Tom. "I am willing to work hard."

"I think you will succeed. You look like a boy of good habits. Energy, industry, and good habits can accomplish wonders. But I think we are on the point of starting."

Just before the gangplank was drawn in, two persons hastily crossed it.

One was the dark young man who had passed them on the way down to the boat; the other was Milton Graham.

"Mr. Waterbury," said Tom hurriedly, "do you see that man?"

"Yes."

"He is the man that tried to rob me."

"We must be on our guard, then. He may be up to more mischief."

CHAPTER X

ON THE STEAMER

In half an hour the River Belle was on her way. Tom watched the city as it receded from view. He enjoyed this new mode of travel better than riding on the cars. He had never before been on any boat except a ferryboat and congratulated himself on his decision to journey by boat part of the way.

Tom continues his journey on the River Belle ferryboat.

Milton Graham had passed him two or three times, but Tom, though seeing him, had not volunteered recognition. Finding that he must make the first advances, Graham finally stopped short, looked full at our hero, and his face wore a very natural expression of surprise and pleasure.

"Why, Tom, is that you?" he said, offering his hand, which Tom did not appear to see.

"Yes," said our hero coldly.

"I didn't expect to see you here."

"I told you I intended to sail on the River Belle."

"So you did, but I thought you had changed your mind."

It made very little difference to Tom what Mr. Graham thought, and he turned from him to watch the scenery past which the boat was gliding.

"I suppose," continued the young man, "you were surprised to find me gone when you came downstairs to breakfast."

"Yes, I was."

"He resents it because I left him," thought Graham. "I guess I can bring him around."

"The fact was," explained Graham, in a plausible manner, "I went out to call on a friend, meaning to come back to breakfast, but he made me breakfast with him, and when I did return you were gone. I owe you an apology, Tom. I hope you will excuse my unintentional neglect."

"Oh, certainly," said Tom indifferently, "it's of no consequence."

Mr. Graham looked at him sharply. He could not tell whether our hero was aware of his dishonest intentions or not, but as Tom must still have money, which he wanted to secure, he thought it best to ignore his coldness.

"No," said he, "it's of no consequence as long as we have come together again. By the way, have you secured a stateroom?"

"Yes."

"If the other berth is not taken, I should like very much to go in with you," said Graham insinuatingly.

"I have a roommate," said Tom coolly.

"You have? Who is it?" demanded Graham, disappointed.

"That gentleman," answered Tom, pointing out Mr. Nicholas Waterbury.

"Humph! Do you know him?"

"I met him at the Pittsburgh House."

"My young friend," said Graham, with the air of a friendly mentor, "I want to give you a piece of advice."

"Very well."

"Don't be too ready to trust strangers. This Mr. Waterbury may be a very good man, but, on the other hand, he may be a confidence man. Do you understand me?"

"I think so."

"Now, I suppose you have money?"

"A little."

"Take care that he doesn't get possession of it. There are men who go about expressly to fleece inexperienced strangers."

"I suppose you know all about that," Tom could not help saying.

"What do you mean?" demanded Graham suspiciously.

"You are an old traveler and must know all about the sharpers."

"Oh, to be sure," said Graham, immediately dismissing his suspicions. "You couldn't leave your companion, could you, and come into my stateroom?"

"I don't think I could."

"Oh, very well. It's of no consequence. Keep a good lookout for your roommate."

Graham turned away and resumed his walk. Soon Tom saw him in company with the dark young man, to whom reference has already been made.

"Well," said the latter, "how did you make out with the boy?"

"He's offish. I don't know if he suspects me. I wanted to get him into my stateroom, but he has already taken up with another man -- that stout party over there."

"So I suspected. I can tell you something about that man."

"What?"

"He carries six hundred dollars about him."

"You don't say so! How did you find out?"

"I overheard him telling the boy so."

"That's important news. The boy must have a couple of hundred, or thereabouts, as he is on his way to California."

"Eight hundred dollars together! That would make a good haul."

"So it would, but it won't be easy to get it."

While this conversation was going on Tom informed Mr. Waterbury of what had passed between Graham and himself.

"So he warned you against me, did he?" said Mr. Waterbury laughingly.

"Yes, he thought I would be safer in his company."

"If you want to exchange, I will retire," said Mr. Waterbury, smiling.

"Thank you; I would rather not. I am glad I met you, or he might have managed to get in with me."

It was not long before they came to a landing. It was a small river village, whose neat white houses, with here and there one of greater pretensions, presented an attractive appearance. A lady and her daughter came on board here. The lady was dressed in black and appeared to be a widow. The girl was perhaps fourteen years of age, with a bright, attractive face. Two trunks were put on the boat with them, and as they were the only passengers from this landing, Tom inferred that they were their property.

"That's quite a pretty girl," said Mr. Waterbury.

"Yes," answered Tom.

"You ought to get acquainted with her," said Mr. Waterbury jocosely.

"Perhaps," said Tom shyly, "you will get acquainted with them, and then you can introduce me."

"You are quite sharp," said Mr. Waterbury, laughing. "However, your hint is a good one. I may act upon it."

It happened, however, that Tom required no introduction. As the lady and her daughter walked across the deck, to occupy some desirable seats on the other side, the former dropped a kid glove, which Tom, espying, hastened forward and, picking up, politely tendered to the owner.

"You are very kind," said the lady, in a pleasant voice. "I am much obliged."

"Mama is quite in the habit of dropping her gloves," said the young girl, with a smiling glance at Tom. "I really think she does it on purpose."

"Then, perhaps, I had better keep nearby to pick them up," said Tom.

"Really, Jennie," said her mother, "you are giving the young gentleman a strange impression of me."

"Well, mama, you know you dropped your gloves in the street the last time you were in Pittsburgh, but there was no gentleman to pick them up, so I had to. Are you going to Cincinnati?" she asked, turning to Tom.

"Yes, and farther; I am going to California," replied Tom.

"Dear me, you will be quite a traveler. I wish I were going to California."

"You wouldn't like to go there on the same business that I am."

"What is that?"

"I am going to dig gold."

"I don't know. I suppose it isn't girl's work, but if I saw any gold about, I should like to dig for it. Is that your father that was standing by you?"

"No," answered Tom. "I hadn't met him till yesterday. We were staying at the same hotel in Pittsburgh."

"He seems like quite a nice old gentleman."

Mr. Waterbury was not over fifty, but to the young girl he seemed an old gentleman.

"I find him very pleasant."

There was a seat next to Jennie, and Tom ventured to occupy it.

"What is your name?" asked the young lady sociably.

"Thomas Nelson, but most people call me Tom."

"My name is Jane Watson, but everybody calls me Jennie."

"That is much prettier than Jane."

"So I think. Jane seems old-maidish, don't you think so?"

"Are you afraid of becoming an old maid?" asked Tom, smiling.

"Awfully. I wouldn't be an old maid for anything. My school teacher is an old maid. She's horribly prim. She won't let us laugh, or talk, or anything."

"I don't think you'll grow up like that."

"I hope not."

The sociable Jennie Watson

"How you run on, Jennie!" said her mother. "What will this young gentleman think of you?"

"Nothing very bad, I hope," said Jennie, smiling archly on Tom. "I suppose," she continued, addressing him, "I ought to be very quiet and reserved, as you are a stranger."

"I hope you won't be," said Tom heartily.

"Then I won't. Somehow you don't seem like a stranger. You look a good deal like a cousin of mine. I suppose that is the reason."

So they chatted on for an hour or more. Jennie was very vivacious and occasionally droll, and Tom enjoyed her company. The mother saw that our hero was well-behaved and gentlemanly, and she made no objection to the sudden intimacy.

CHAPTER XI

THE FIRST DAY ON THE RIVER

About half-past twelve lunch was announced.

"I hope you'll sit next to us, Tom," said Jennie Watson.

"I will, if I can."

It happened that Milton Graham entered the saloon at the same time with the new friends. He took the seat next to Jennie, much to that young lady's annoyance.

"Will you be kind enough to take the next seat?" she asked. "That young gentleman is to sit next to me."

"I am sorry to resign the pleasure, but anything to oblige," said Graham. "Tom, I congratulate you," he continued, with a disagreeable smile.

"Thank you," said our hero briefly.

"He calls you Tom. Does he know you?" inquired Jennie, in a low voice.

"I made his acquaintance yesterday for the first time."

"I don't like his looks; do you?"

"Wait till after dinner, and I will tell you," said Tom, fearing that Graham would hear.

Milton Graham saw that Jennie was pretty and desired to make her acquaintance.

"Tom," said he -- for he sat on the other side of our hero -- "won't you introduce me to your young lady friend?"

Tom was not well versed in etiquette, but his good sense told him that he ought to ask Jennie's permission first.

"If Miss Watson is willing," he said, and asked her the question.

Jennie was not aware of Graham's real character, and she gave permission. She was perhaps a little too ready to make new acquaintances.

"Do you enjoy this mode of travel, Miss Watson?" said Graham, after the introduction.

"Oh, yes. I think it very pleasant."

"I suppose you wouldn't like the ocean as well. I went to Havana last winter -- on business for my father -- and had a very rough passage. The steamer pitched and tossed, making us all miserably seasick."

"I shouldn't like that."

"I don't think you would, but we businessmen must not regard such things."

Tom listened to him with incredulity. Only the day before he would have put full confidence in his statement, but he had learned a lesson, thanks to Graham himself.

"How far are you going, Miss Watson?" continued Graham.

"To Cincinnati. My mother and I are going to live there."

"It is a very pleasant city. I have often been there -- on business."

"What is your business, Mr. Graham?" Tom could not help asking.

"I see you are a Yankee," said Graham, smiling. "Yankees are very inquisitive -- always asking questions."

"Are you a Yankee, Mr. Graham?" asked Jennie. "You asked me where I was going."

"A fair hit," said Graham. "No, I am not a Yankee. I am a native of New York."

"And I of New Jersey," said Tom.

"Oh, you are a foreigner then," said Graham. "We always call Jerseymen foreigners."

"It is a stupid joke, I think," said Tom, who was loyal to his native state.

"You didn't answer Tom's question," said Jennie, who was a very straightforward young lady.

"Oh, my father is a commission merchant," answered Graham.

"What does he deal in?"

"Articles too numerous to mention. Tom, will you pass me the potatoes?"

Lunch was soon over, and the passengers went upon deck. Graham lit a cigar.

"Have a cigar, Tom?" he said.

"No, thank you. I don't smoke."

"You'll soon learn. I'll see you again soon."

"Tom," said Jennie, "tell me about this Mr. Graham. What do you know about him?"

"I don't like to tell what I know," said Tom hesitating.

"But I want you to. You introduced me, you know."

"What I know is not to his advantage. I don't like to talk against a man."

"You needn't mind telling me."

On reflection Tom decided that he ought to tell what he knew, for he felt that Jennie ought to be put on her guard against a man whom he did not consider a suitable acquaintance for her.

"Very well," said he, "if you promise not to let him know that I have told you."

"I promise."

"He was my roommate last night at the Pittsburgh House," said Tom, in a low voice. "During the night he tried to rob me."

"You don't say so!" cried Jennie, in round-eyed wonder.

"I will tell you the particulars."

This Tom did. Jennie listened with indignation.

"But I don't understand," she said. "Why should the son of a merchant need to rob a boy like you? He looks as if he had plenty of money."

"So I thought, but the hotel clerk told me that sharpers often appeared like this Mr. Graham, if that is his name."

"How strange it seems!" said Jennie. "I wish you hadn't introduced me."

"I didn't want to, but he asked, and at the table I couldn't give my reasons for refusing."

"My dear child," said her mother, "you are too ready to form new acquaintances. Let this be a lesson for you."

"But some new acquaintances are nice," pleaded Jennie. "Isn't Tom a new acquaintance?"

"I will make an exception in his favor," said Mrs. Watson, smiling pleasantly.

"Thank you," said Tom. "How do you know that I am not a pickpocket?" he continued, addressing Jennie.

"As I have only ten cents in my pocket I will trust you," said the young lady merrily. "I'd trust you with any amount, Tom," she added impulsively.

"Thank you for your good opinion, Miss Jennie."

"Don't call me Miss Jennie. If you do, I'll call you Mr. Tom."

"I shouldn't know myself by that title. Then I'll call you Jennie."

"I wish you were going to live in Cincinnati," said the young lady. "It would be nice to have you come and see us."

"I should like it, but I mustn't think so much of pleasure as business."

"Like Mr. Graham."

"I must work hard at the mines. I suppose I shall look pretty rough when I am there."

"When you've made your pile, Tom -- that's what they call it, isn't it? -- you'll come back, won't you?"

"Yes."

"You must stop in Cincinnati on your way home."

"I wouldn't know where to find you."

"I will give you our address before we part. But that will be some time yet."

About this time Graham, who had finished smoking his cigar, strolled back.

"Miss Watson," said he, "don't you feel like having a promenade?"

"Yes," said Jennie suddenly. "Tom, come walk with me."

Our hero readily accepted the invitation, and the two walked up and down the deck.

"That's what I call a snub," said Graham's friend, the dark-complexioned young man, who was within hearing.

Graham's face was dark with anger.

"Curse her impudence -- and his too!" he muttered. "I should like to wring the boy's neck."

"He can't help it, if the girl prefers his company," said the other, rather enjoying Graham's mortification.

"I'll punish him all the same."

By this time Tom and Jennie were near him again, on their return.

"You don't treat me with much ceremony, Miss Watson," said Graham, with an evil smile.

"My mother doesn't like me to make too many acquaintances," said Jennie demurely.

"She is very prudent," sneered Graham. "You have known your present companion quite a long time."

"I hope to know him a long time," said the young lady promptly. "Let's continue our walk, Tom."

In discomfiture which he was unable to hide, Graham walked away.

"Evidently, Graham, you are no match for those two youngsters," said his friend in amusement, which Graham did not share.

Graham did not reply but seemed moody and preoccupied.

Tom and his companion noticed Graham's displeasure, but they felt indifferent to it. They had no desire to continue his acquaintance. Our hero introduced Mr. Waterbury to his new friends, and this gentleman, who was a thorough gentleman, except on the rare occasion when he yielded to the temptation of strong drink, made a favorable impression upon both.

So the day passed. Tom enjoyed it thoroughly. The river banks afforded a continuous panorama, while the frequent stops gave him an opportunity of observing the different towns in detail. Two or three times he went ashore, accompanied by Jennie, and remained till the steamer was ready to start.

Finally night came, and one by one the weary passengers retired to rest.

"Good night, Tom," said Jennie Watson. "Be up early in the morning."

"So as to get an appetite for breakfast?" asked Tom, with a smile.

"I think we shall both have appetites enough, but it will be pleasant to breathe the fresh morning air."

Tom promised to get up, if he wakened in time.

"If you don't mind, I will occupy the lower berth," said Mr. Waterbury. "I can't climb as well as you."

"All right, sir. It makes no difference to me."

CHAPTER XII

NO. 61 AND NO. 62

The stateroom was small, as most staterooms on river boats are. There appeared to be no means of ventilation. Mr. Waterbury was a stout man and inclined to be short-breathed. After an hour he rose and opened the door, so as to leave it slightly ajar. With the relief thus afforded he was able to go to sleep, and sleep soundly. Tom was already asleep and knew nothing of what had happened.

The number of the stateroom was 61. Directly opposite was 62, occupied by Milton Graham and his companion.

If Graham did not go to sleep it was because his brain was busily scheming how to obtain possession of the money belonging to his neighbors.

"Won't your key fit?" asked Vincent, for this was the name of the dark-complexioned young man.

"No use, even if it does. Of course they will lock it inside and probably leave the key in the lock."

About midnight, Graham, who had not fully undressed, having merely taken off his coat, got up, and, opening the door, peered out. To his surprise and joy he saw that the door of No. 61 was ajar. He at first thought of rousing Vincent, who was asleep, but a selfish thought suggested itself. If he did this, he must share with Vincent anything he might succeed in stealing; if not, he could keep it all himself.

He left his stateroom silently, and looked cautiously around him. No one seemed to be stirring in the cabin. Next he stepped across and, opening wider the door of 61, looked in. The two inmates were, to all appearances, sleeping soundly.

"So far, so good," he said to himself.

He stepped in, moderating even his breathing, and took up a pair of pants which lay on a chair. They belonged to Mr. Waterbury, for Tom had merely taken off his coat and lain down as he was. His belt of gold he therefore found it unnecessary to take off.

Graham saw at once, from the size of the pants, that they must belong to the elder passenger. This suited him, however, as he knew from Vincent's information that Mr. Waterbury had six hundred dollars, and Tom could not be supposed to have anything like this sum. He felt eagerly in the pockets, and to his great joy his hand came in contact with a pocketbook. He drew it out without ceremony. It was a comfortable-looking wallet, fairly bulging with bills.

"He's got all his money inside," thought Graham, delighted. "What a fool he must be to leave it so exposed -- with his door open, too!"

At this moment Graham heard a stir in the lower berth. There was no time to wait. He glided out of the room and reentered his own stateroom. Immediately after his departure Mr. Waterbury, who had awakened in time to catch sight of his receding figure, rose in his berth and drew toward him the garment which Graham had rifled. He felt in the pocket and discovered that the wallet had been taken.

Instead of making a fuss, he smiled quietly and said, "Just as I expected. I wonder if they have robbed Tom, too," he said to himself.

He rose, closed the door, and then shook Tom with sufficient energy to awaken him.

"Who's there?" asked Tom, in some bewilderment, as he opened his eyes.

"It's I -- Mr. Waterbury."

"Is it morning? Have we arrived?"

"No, it is about midnight."

"Is there anything the matter?"

"I want you to see if you have been robbed.'"

Tom was broad awake in an instant.

"Robbed!" he exclaimed, in alarm. He felt for his belt and was relieved.

"No," he answered. "What makes you ask?"

"Because I have had a wallet taken. It makes me laugh when I think of it."

"Makes you laugh!" repeated Tom, under the transient impression that his companion was insane. "Why should you laugh at the loss of your money?"

"I saw the thief sneak out of the stateroom," continued Mr. Waterbury, "but I didn't interfere with him."

"You didn't!" said Tom, completely mystified. "I would. Did you see who it was?"

"Yes, it was your friend and late roommate."

"Mr. Graham?"

"As he calls himself. I don't suppose he has any rightful claim to the name."

"Surely, Mr. Waterbury, you are not going to let him keep the money," said Tom energetically. "I'll go with you, and make him give it up. Where is his stateroom?"

"Just opposite -- No. 62."

"We had better go at once," said Tom, sitting up in his berth.

"Oh, no. He's welcome to all there is in the pocketbook."

"Wasn't there anything in it?"

"It was stuffed full."

Tom was more than ever convinced that his roommate was crazy. He had heard that misfortune sometimes affected a man's mind, and he was inclined to think that here was a case in point.

"You'll get it back," said he soothingly. "Graham can't get off the boat. We will report the matter to the captain."

"I don't care whether I get it back or not," said Mr. Waterbury.

Tom looked so confused and bewildered that his companion felt called upon to end the mystification.

"I know what is in your mind," he said, smiling. "You think I am crazy."

"I don't understand how you can take your loss so coolly, sir."

"Then I will explain. That wallet was a dummy."

"A what, sir?"

"A sham -- a pretense. My pocketbook and money are safe under my pillow. The wallet taken by your friend was filled with imitation greenbacks -- in reality, business circulars of a firm in Marietta."

Tom saw it all now.

"It's a capital joke," he said, laughing. "I'd like to see how Graham looks when he discovers the value of his prize."

"He will look green and feel greener, I suspect," chuckled Mr. Waterbury. "You are certain you have lost nothing, Tom?"

"Perfectly certain, sir."

"Then we won't trouble ourselves about what has happened. I fancy, however, it will be best to keep our own door locked for the remainder of the night, even at the risk of suffocation."

"That's a capital trick of yours, Mr. Waterbury," said Tom admiringly.

"It has more than once saved me from robbery. I have occasion to travel considerably and so am more or less exposed."

"I wonder if Graham will discover the cheat before morning."

"I doubt it. The staterooms are dark, and the imitation is so good that on casual inspection the strips of paper will appear to be genuine greenbacks."

Mr. Waterbury retired to his berth and was soon asleep again. Tom, as he lay awake, from time to time laughed to himself, as he thought of Graham's coming disappointment, and he congratulated himself that he and that young man were no longer roommates.

When Graham returned to his stateroom Vincent, who was a light sleeper, was aroused by the slight noise he made.

"Are you up, Graham?" he asked.

"Yes. I got up a minute."

"Have you been out of the stateroom?"

"Yes."

"What for?"

"To get a glass of water."

There was a vessel of water in the cabin, and this seemed plausible enough.

"Any chance of doing anything tonight?"

"No, I think not."

Vincent sank back on his pillow, and Graham got back into his berth. Quietly he drew the wallet from his pocket, in which he had placed it, and eagerly opened it. The huge roll of bills was a pleasant and welcome sight.

"There's all of six hundred dollars here!" he said to himself. "I mustn't let Vincent know that I have them."

It occurred to Graham that, of course, Mr. Waterbury would proclaim his loss in the morning, and it also occurred to him that he might be able to fasten suspicion upon Tom, who, as his roommate, would naturally have the best chance to commit the robbery. One thing might criminate him -- the discovery of the wallet upon his person. He therefore waited till Vincent was once more asleep and, getting up softly, made his way to the deck. He drew the bills from the wallet, put them in an inside pocket, and threw the wallet into the river.

"Now I'm safe," he muttered, with a sigh of relief. "The money may be found on me, but no one can prove it is not my own."

He gained his berth without again awakening his companion.

"A pretty good night's work!" he said to himself, in quiet exultation. "Alone I have succeeded, while Vincent lies in stupid sleep. He is no match for me, much as he thinks of himself. I have stolen a march upon him this time."

It is not in accordance with our ideas of the fitness of things that a man who has committed a midnight robbery should be able to sleep tranquilly for the balance of the night, but it is at any rate certain that Graham slept soundly till his roommate awakened him in the morning.

"Rouse up, Graham," he said. "Breakfast is nearly ready."

"Is it?" asked Graham.

"Instead of sleeping there, you ought to be thinking how we can make a forced loan from our acquaintances in 61."

"To be sure," said Graham, smiling. "I am rather stupid about such things. Have you any plan to suggest?"

"You seem very indifferent all at once," said Vincent.

"Not at all. If you think of anything practical I am your man."

He longed to get rid of Vincent, in order to have an opportunity of counting his roll of bills.

CHAPTER XIII

GRAHAM'S DISAPPOINTMENT

Milton Graham, on reaching a place where he could do so unobserved, drew from his pocket the roll of bills, with a smile of exultation. But the smile faded, and it was succeeded by a look of dismay, when he recognized the worthlessness of his booty. An oath rose to his lips, and he thrust the roll back into his pocket, as he noticed the approach of a passenger.

"It's a cursed imposition!" he muttered to himself, and he really felt that he had been wronged by Mr. Waterbury.

"What are you doing out here, Graham?" asked Vincent, for it was his confederate who approached.

"Nothing in particular. Why?" responded Graham.

"What makes you look so glum?"

"Do I look glum?"

"You look as if you had but one friend in the world, and you were about to lose him."

"That may be true enough," muttered Graham.

"Come, man, don't look so downcast."

"I'm out of luck, and out of cash, Vincent."

"We're both in the same boat, as far as that goes, but that isn't going to last. How about our stout friend? Can't we make him contribute to our necessities?"

"I don't believe he's got any money."

"No? Why, I heard him tell the boy he had six hundred dollars."

"Where does he keep it?"

"In his pocketbook probably."

"Will you oblige me by stating how we are going to get hold of it?"

"I look to you for that."

"He's too careful. I leave you to try your hand."

"Let me go in to breakfast. There's nothing like a full stomach to suggest ideas."

So the two went to the breakfast table, and Graham, in spite of his disappointment, managed to eat a hearty meal.

An hour later Mr. Waterbury and Tom were standing on deck, conversing with Jennie Watson and her mother, when Graham and Vincent approached arm in arm. As soon as they were within hearing distance Mr. Waterbury purposely remarked, "By the way, Mrs. Watson, I met with a loss last night."

"Indeed!" returned the lady.

Graham was about to push on, not wishing Vincent to hear the disclosure, as it might awaken his suspicions, but the latter's curiosity was aroused.

"Wait, Graham," he said, and Graham, against his will, was compelled to slacken his pace.

"A man entered my stateroom during the night, and stole a wallet from my coat pocket."

Graham changed color a little, and Vincent seemed amazed.

"Did you hear that, Graham?" he asked.

"Yes."

"What does it mean?"

"How can I tell?"

"I hope you did not lose much," said Mrs. Watson, in a tone of sympathy.

"I lost the wallet," said Mr. Waterbury, laughing.

"Was there nothing in it?"

"It was full of bills."

Vincent looked at Graham with new-born suspicion, but Graham looked indifferent.

"It appears to me that you take the loss cheerfully," said Mrs. Watson, puzzled.

"I have reason to. The fact is, I was prepared for the visit and had filled the wallet with bogus bills. I fancy they won't do my visitor much good."

The lady smiled.

"You were fortunate, Mr. Waterbury," said she. "Do you suspect any one of the theft?"

"I know pretty well who robbed me," returned Mr. Waterbury, and he suffered his glance to rest on Graham, who seemed in a hurry to get away.

"Come along, Vincent," he said sharply.

Vincent obeyed. Light dawned upon him, and he determined to verify his suspicions.

"Graham," said he, in a low voice, "you did this."

"Did what?"

"You got that wallet."

Graham concluded that he might as well make a clean breast of it, since it had become a matter of necessity.

"Well," said he, "suppose I did?"

"You were not going to let me know of it," said Vincent suspiciously.

"That is true. I was ashamed of having been imposed upon."

"When did you find out that the money was bogus?"

"Immediately."

"If it had been good, would you have shared with me honorably?"

"Of course. What do you take me for?"

Vincent was silent. He did not believe his companion. He suspected that the latter had intended to steal a march on him.

"You might have told me of it," he continued, in a tone of dissatisfaction.

"There was no need to say anything, as there was nothing to divide."

"Have you got the wallet with you now?"

"No, I threw it overboard."

"And the bills?"

"You may have them all, if you like."

"Come into the stateroom, where we can be unobserved, and show them to me."

Graham complied with his suggestion.

"It would have been a good haul if they had been genuine," said Vincent, as he unfolded the roll.

"Yes, but they are not; worse luck!"

"I didn't give the old fellow credit for being so sharp."

"Nor I. There's more in him than I supposed there was."

"Well, what is to be done?"

"Nothing. The old man is on his guard, and, besides, he suspects me. He was probably awake when I entered the stateroom. He and the boy have probably laughed over it together. I hate that boy."

"Why?"

"Because he is a green country boy, and yet he has succeeded in thwarting me. I am ashamed whenever I think of it."

"Would you like to play a trick on him in turn?"

"Yes."

"Then give me this roll of bills."

"What do you want to do with them?"

"Put them in his pocket."

"Can you do it unobserved?"

"Yes. The fact is, Graham, I served an apprenticeship as a pickpocket, and flatter myself I still have some dexterity in that line."

"Very well, it will be some satisfaction, and if the old man didn't see me enter the stateroom, he may be brought to believe that the boy robbed him. If that could be, I should feel partly compensated for my disappointment. I should like to get that boy into trouble."

"Consider it done, so far as I am concerned. Now let us separate, so as to avoid suspicion."

Vincent began to pace the deck in a leisurely manner, in each case passing near Tom, who was still engaged in conversation with Jennie Watson and her mother. For a time he was unable to effect his purpose, as our hero was sitting down. But after a while Tom rose and stood with his back to Vincent. He wore a sack coat, with side pockets. This was favorable to Vincent, who, as he passed, adroitly slipped the bills into one of them, without attracting the attention of our hero.

Presently Tom thrust his hand into his pocket mechanically. They encountered the bills. In surprise he drew them out and looked at them in amazement.

"What's that, Tom?" asked Jennie, with great curiosity.

"It looks like money," answered Tom, not yet understanding what had happened.

"You seem to be rich."

"By gracious! -- it's Mr. Waterbury's money," exclaimed Tom. Then he colored, as it flashed upon him that its presence in his pocket might arouse suspicion. "I don't see how it got there," he continued, in a bewildered way.

Just then Mr. Waterbury came up and was made acquainted with the discovery.

"I don't know what you'll think, Mr. Waterbury," said Tom, coloring. "I haven't the slightest idea how the money came in my pocket."

"I have," said Mr. Waterbury quietly.

Tom looked at him to discover whether he was under suspicion.

"The companion of your friend Graham slipped it into your pocket. He was very quick and adroit, but I detected him. He wanted to throw suspicion upon you."

"It is lucky you saw him, sir."

"Why?"

"You might have suspected me."

"My dear boy, don't trouble yourself about that. No circumstantial evidence will shake my confidence in your integrity."

"Thank you, sir," said Tom gratefully.

"What a wicked man to play a trick on you, Tom!" exclaimed Jennie indignantly.

"I see there is somebody else who has confidence in you, Tom," said Mr. Waterbury, smiling.

"I'd like to give him a piece of my mind."

"I am ready to forgive him," said Mr. Waterbury, "as he has restored the money. It will do as a bait for the next thief."

CHAPTER XIV

COMING TO AN UNDERSTANDING

"I believe, Tom," said Mr. Waterbury, "that I will come to an understanding with these officious acquaintances of yours. I will intimate to them that their persecution must cease."

"Will they mind what you say, sir?"

"I think they will," answered his friend quietly.

Graham and Vincent were standing together, and apart from the rest of the passengers, when Mr. Waterbury approached them.

"A word with you, gentlemen," said he gravely.

"I don't know you, sir," blustered Vincent.

"Perhaps not. Permit me to remark that I have no special desire for your acquaintance."

"Then why do you take the liberty of addressing me?"

"I rather admire the fellow's impudence," said Mr. Waterbury to himself.

"   Are you associated with this gentleman?" he asked, indicating Graham.

"We are friends."

"Then I will address an inquiry to him. I am not in the habit of receiving calls in my stateroom during the hours of sleep."

"I don't understand you, sir," said Milton Graham, with hauteur.

"Oh, yes, you do, unless your memory is singularly defective. Our staterooms are close together. You entered mine last night."

"You must have been dreaming."

"If so, I was dreaming with my eyes open. Perhaps it was in my dreams that I saw you extract a wallet from my coat pocket."

"Do you mean to insult me, sir?" demanded Graham.

"Really, sir, your remarks are rather extraordinary," chimed in Vincent.

"Do you mean to say that I robbed you?" demanded Graham, confident in the knowledge that the booty was not on his person.

"I find a wallet missing. That speaks for itself."

"Let me suggest that your roommate probably took it," said Vincent.

"Extremely probable," said Graham. "He roomed with me in Pittsburgh, and I caught him at my pockets during the night."

"Did you ever hear the fable of the wolf and the lamb, Mr. Graham?" asked Mr. Waterbury.

"Can't say I have."

"It's of no consequence. I am reminded of it, however."

"Come to think of it," said Vincent, "I saw the boy with a roll of bills. You had better search him. If he is innocent, he can't object."

"I see your drift," returned Mr. Waterbury, after a pause. "I saw you thrust the bills into his pocket, as he stood with his back turned, conversing with one of the passengers. It was very skillfully done, but I saw it."

Vincent started, for he had supposed himself unobserved.

"I see you are determined to insult us," he said. "I will charitably conclude that you are drunk."

"I can't be so charitable with you, sir. I believe you are a pair of precious scoundrels, who, if you had your deserts, would be in the penitentiary instead of at large."

"I have a mind to knock you down," said Vincent angrily.

As Vincent was several inches shorter and much slighter than the person whom he threatened, this menace sounded rather ridiculous.

"You are at liberty to try it," said the latter, smiling. "First, however, let me warn you that, if you continue to annoy us, it will be at your peril. If you remain quiet I shall leave you alone. Otherwise I will make known your true character to the captain and passengers, and you will undoubtedly be set ashore when we reach the next landing. I have the honor to wish you good morning."

"It strikes me, Graham," said Vincent, as Mr. Waterbury left them, "that we have tackled the wrong passenger."

"I believe you are right," said Graham. "Just my luck."

"There isn't much use in staying on the boat. He will keep a good lookout for us."

"True, but I don't want to give up the boy."

"He is under the guardianship of this determined old party."

"They will separate at Cincinnati."

"Well?"

"He has money enough to take him to California. He is worth following up."

"Then you are in favor of going on to Cincinnati?"

"By all means."

"Very well. There are always chances of making an honest penny in a large city."

"Money or no money, I want to get even with the boy."

So the worthy pair decided to go on to Cincinnati.

CHAPTER XV

THE ALLEGHANY HOUSE

It was a bright, sunny morning when the River Belle touched her pier at Cincinnati. The passengers gathered on deck and discussed their plans. In one group were Tom, Mr. Waterbury, Jennie Watson and her mother.

"I am sorry you are going to leave us, Tom," said Jennie. "I shall feel awfully lonely."

"So shall I," said Tom.

"What's the use of going to that hateful California? Why can't you stay here with us?"

"Business before pleasure, Jennie," said her mother. "You mustn't forget that Tom has his fortune to make."

"I wish he could make it in Cincinnati, mother."

"So do I, but I must admit that California presents a better prospect just at present. You are both young, and I hope we may meet Tom in a few years."

"When I have made my pile," suggested Tom.

"Precisely."

"You won't go right on, Tom, will you?" asked Jennie. "You'll stay here a day or two."

"Yes. I should like to see something of Cincinnati."

"And you'll call on us?"

"I shall be very happy to do so. Where are you going to stay?"

"At the Burnet House. Won't you come there, too?"

"Is it a high-priced hotel?"

"I believe it is."

"Then I can't afford to stay there, but I can call on you all the same."

"Stay there as my guest, Tom," said Mr. Waterbury cordially. "It shall not cost you anything."

"Thank you, sir. You are very kind, but I don't like to accept unnecessary favors. I will put up at some cheap hotel and call upon you both."

"You would be heartily welcome, my boy," said Mr. Waterbury.

"I don't doubt it, sir, and the time may come when I will gladly accept your kindness," replied Tom.

"But now you mean to have your own way, is that it, Tom?"

"You won't be offended, sir?"

"On the contrary, I respect you for your manly independence. You won't forget that I am your friend?"

"I don't want to forget that, sir."

So it happened that while Mrs. Watson, Jennie and Mr. Waterbury registered at the Burnet House, Tom, carpetbag in hand, walked through the streets till he came to a plain inn, bearing the name Alleghany House. It is not now in existence, having given way to an imposing business block.

"That looks as if it might suit my purse," thought Tom.

He walked in and, approaching the desk, inquired, "How much do you charge at this hotel?"

"A dollar a day," answered the clerk. "Will you have a room?"

"Yes, sir."

"Please register your name." Tom did so.

"Cato," called the clerk -- summoning a colored boy, about Tom's size -- "take this young man to No. 18."

"All right, sar," said Cato, showing his ivories.

"When do you have lunch?" asked Tom.

"One o'clock."

Preceded by Cato, Tom walked upstairs and was ushered into a small, dingy room on the second floor. There was a single window, looking through dingy panes upon a back yard. There was a general air of cheerlessness and discomfort, but at any rate it was larger than the stateroom on the River Belle.

"Is this the best room you have?" asked Tom, not very favorably impressed.

"Oh, no, sar," answered Cato. "If your wife was with you, sar, we'd give you a scrumptious room, 'bout twice as big."

"I didn't bring my wife along, Cato," said Tom, amused. "Are you married?"

"Not yet, sar," answered his colored guide, with a grin.

"I think we can wait till we are a little older."

"Reckon so, sar."

"Just bring up a little water, Cato. I feel in need of washing."

"Dirt don't show on me," said Cato, with a guffaw.

"I suppose you do wash, now and then, don't you?"

"Yes, sar, sometimes," answered Cato equivocally.

When Tom had completed his washing he found that it was but ten o'clock. He accordingly went downstairs, intending to see a little of the city before lunch.

CHAPTER XVI

THE EVENTS OF A MORNING

Graham and Vincent had kept quiet during the latter part of the voyage. They had a wholesome fear of Mr. Waterbury and kept aloof from him and Tom. They even exchanged their stateroom for one at a different part of the boat. All was satisfactory to Tom and his companion.

When the worthy pair reached Cincinnati they were hard up. Their united funds amounted to but seven dollars, and it seemed quite necessary that they should find the means of replenishing their purses somewhere. They managed to ascertain that Tom and his friend were going to separate, and this afforded them satisfaction, since it made their intentions upon our hero more feasible. At a distance they followed Tom to the Alleghany House and themselves took lodgings at a small, cheap tavern nearby. Like Tom, they set out soon after their arrival in quest of adventure.

"We must strike a vein soon, Graham," said Vincent, "or we shall be in a tight place."

"That's so," answered Graham.

"Thus far our trip hasn't paid very well. It's been all outgo and no income."

"You're right, partner, but don't give up the ship," responded Graham, whose spirits returned, now that he was on dry land. "I've been in the same straits about once a month for the last five years."

"I've known you for three years, Graham, and, so far as my knowledge extends, I can attest the truth of what you say. By the way, you never say anything of your life before that date."

A shadow passed over Graham's face.

"Because I don't care to think of it; I never talk of it," he said.

"Pshaw, man, we all of us have some ugly secrets. Suppose we confide in each other. Tell me your story, and I will tell you mine. It won't change my opinion of you."

"Probably not," said Graham. "Well, there is no use in holding back. For this once I will go back to the past. Five years ago I was a favorite in society. One day an acquaintance introduced me into a gambling house, and I tried my hand successfully. I went out with fifty dollars more than I brought in. It was an unlucky success, for it made me a frequent visitor. All my surplus cash found a market there, and when that was exhausted I borrowed from my employer."

"Without his knowledge?"

"Of course. For six months I evaded discovery. Then I was detected. My friends interceded and saved me from the penitentiary, but I lost my job and was required to leave the city. I went to New York, tried to obtain a position there, failed, and then adopted my present profession. I need not tell you the rest."

"My dear friend, I think I know the rest pretty well. But don't look sober. A fig for the past. What's the odds, as long as you're happy?"

"Are you happy?" inquired Graham.

"As long as I'm flush," answered Vincent, shrugging his shoulders. "I'm nearly dead-broke now, and of course I am miserable. However, my story comes next in order. I was a bank teller, appropriated part of the funds of the bank, fled with it, spent it, and then became an ornament to our common profession."

"Where was the bank?"

"In Canada. I haven't been there since. The climate don't suit me. It's bleak, but I fear it might prove too hot for me. Now we know each other."

"You don't allow it to worry you, Vincent," said Graham.

"No, I don't. Why should I? I let the dead past bury its dead, as Longfellow says, and act in the living present. That reminds me, we ought to be at work. I have a proposal to make. We won't hunt in couples, but separate, and each will try to bring home something to help the common fund. Is it agreed?"

"Yes."

"Au revoir, then!"

"That fellow has no conscience," thought Graham. "Mine is callous, but he goes beyond me. Perhaps he is the better off."

Graham shook off his transient dull spirits and walked on, keeping a sharp lookout for a chance to fleece somebody. In front of a railroad ticket office he espied a stolid-looking German, who was trying to read the placard in the window.

Graham approached him and said politely, "My friend, perhaps I can help you. Are you thinking of buying a railroad ticket?"

The German turned, and his confidence was inspired by the friendly interest of Graham's manner.

"I go to Minnesota," he said, "where my brother live."

"Exactly, and you want a ticket to go there?"

"Yes, I want a ticket. Do they sell him here?"

"No," said Graham. "That is, they do sell tickets here, but they ask too much."

"I will not pay too much," said the German, shaking his head decisively.

"Of course not; I will take you to a cheaper place."

"That is good," said the German, well pleased. "It is luck I meet a friend like you."

"Yes," said Graham, linking his arm in that of his new acquaintance. "I don't like to see a worthy man cheated. Come with me. How much money have you?"

This inquiry ought to have excited the suspicions of the German, but he was trustful and answered promptly, "Two hundred dollar."

Graham's eyes sparkled.

"If I could only get the whole of it," he thought. But that didn't seem easy.

They walked through street after street till Graham stopped in front of an office.

"Now," said he, "give me your money, and I will buy the ticket."

"How much money?" asked his new acquaintance.

"I don't know exactly," said Graham carelessly. "Just hand me your pocketbook, and I will pay what is needed."

But here the German's characteristic caution came in.

"I will go with you," he said.

"If you do, I can't get the tickets so cheap. The agent is a friend of mine, and if he thinks it is for me he will give it to me for less. Don't give me all your money. Fifty dollars will do. I will buy the ticket, and bring you the rest of the money."

This seemed plausible enough, and Graham would have got what he asked for, but for the interference of Tom, who had come up just in time to hear Graham's proposal. He had no difficulty in comprehending his purpose.

"Don't give him the money," he said. "He will cheat you."

Both Graham and his intended victim wheeled round and looked at our hero.

"Clear out of here, you young vagabond!" said Graham angrily.

"This man wants to cheat you," persisted Tom. "Don't give him your money."

The bewildered foreigner looked from one to the other.

"This is no ticket office," said Tom. "I will lead you to one, and you shall buy a ticket for yourself."

"He wants to swindle you," said Graham quickly.

"You shall keep your money in your own hands," said Tom. "I don't want it."

"I go with you, my young friend," said the German, convinced by Tom's honest face. "The other man may be all right, but I go with you."

Graham protested in vain. His victim went off with Tom, who saw that he was provided with the ticket he wanted. His new friend tried to force a dollar upon him, but this Tom steadily refused.

"I'll get even with you yet!" said Graham furiously, but our hero was not disturbed by this menace.

Vincent, meantime, was making a tour of observation, ready for any adventure that might put an honest or dishonest penny into his pocket. About half an hour later he found himself on the leading retail street in Cincinnati. In front of him walked a lady, fashionably attired, holding a mother-of-pearl portemonnaie carelessly in her hand. He brushed by her, and at the same moment the pocketbook was snatched from her hand.

The lady screamed and instinctively clutched Vincent by the arm.

"This man has robbed me, I think," she said. The crowd began to gather about Vincent, and he saw that he was cornered. Among the crowd, unluckily for himself, was Tom. By a skilful movement Vincent thrust the portemonnaie into our hero's pocket.

"You are mistaken, madam," he said coolly. "I saw that boy take your money."

Instantly two men seized Tom.

"Search him," said Vincent, "and see if I am not right."

The portemonnaie was taken from Tom's pocket, amid the hootings of the crowd.

"So young, and yet so wicked!" said the lady regretfully.

"I didn't take the money, madam," protested Tom, his face scarlet with surprise and mortification.

"Don't believe him, ma'am. I saw him take it," said Vincent virtuously.

Poor Tom looked from one to another, but all faces were unfriendly. It was a critical time for him.

CHAPTER XVII

TOM'S ARREST

To one who is scrupulously honest a sudden charge of dishonesty is almost overwhelming. Now, Tom was honest, not so much because he had been taught that honesty was a virtue, as by temperament and instinct. Yet here he saw himself surrounded by hostile faces, for a crowd soon collected. Not one believed in his innocence, not even the lady, who thought it was such a pity that he was "so young and yet so wicked."

"Will somebody call a policeman?" asked Vincent.

A policeman soon made his appearance. He was a stout, burly man, and pushed his way through the crowd without ceremony.

"What's the row?" he inquired.

"This boy has picked a lady's pocket," exclaimed Vincent.

The officer placed his hand roughly on Tom's shoulder.

"You were a little too smart, young feller!" said he. "You must come along with me."

"I didn't take the money," protested Tom, pale, but in a firm voice.

"That's too thin," said Vincent, with a sneer.

"Yes, it's too thin," repeated two or three in the crowd.

"It's true," said Tom.

"Perhaps you'll tell us how the money came in your pocket," suggested a bystander.

"That man put it in," answered Tom, indicating Vincent.

The latter shrugged his shoulders.

"He says so, because I exposed him," he remarked, turning to the crowd.

"Of course; that's a common game," interposed the policeman.

"Have you any reason for what you say, my boy?" asked a quiet-looking man, with a pleasant face.

"Of course he hasn't," replied Vincent hastily.

"I spoke to the boy, sir."

"I have a reason," answered Tom. "A friend of this man roomed with me at Pittsburgh and during the night tried to rob me. We were both passengers on the River Belle on the last trip. During the trip he entered our stateroom and stole a wallet from my roommate. This man slyly put it into my pocket, in order to escape suspicion."

"It's a lie!" exclaimed Vincent uneasily. "Gentlemen, the boy is very artful, and the greatest liar out."

"Of course he is!" assented the policeman. "Come along, young feller!"

"Wait a minute," said the quiet man. "Have you any proof of your statements, my boy, except your own word?"

"Yes, sir. My roommate will tell you the same thing."

"Who is he? Where can he be found?"

"He is Mr. Nicholas Waterbury, of Marietta. He is now at the Burnet House."

"That's all gammon!" said the officer roughly. "Come along. I can't wait here all day."

"Don't be in a hurry, officer," said the quiet man. "I know Mr. Waterbury, and I believe the boy's story is correct."

"It ain't any of your business!" said the officer insolently. "The boy's a thief, and I'm goin' to lock him up."

"Look out, sir!" said the quiet man sternly. "You are overstepping the limits of your duty and asserting what you have no possible means of knowing. There is reason to believe that this man" -- pointing out Vincent -- "is the real thief. I call upon you to arrest him."

"I don't receive no orders from you, sir," said the policeman. "I'm more likely to take you along."

"That's right, officer," said Vincent approvingly. "The man is interfering with you in the exercise of your duty. You have a perfect right to arrest him."

"I have a great mind to," said the officer, who was one of the many who are puffed up by a little brief authority and lose no opportunity of exercising it.

The quiet man did not seem in the least alarmed. He smiled and said, "Perhaps, officer, it might be well for you to inquire my name, before proceeding to arrest me."

"Who are you?" demanded the officer insolently.

"I am Alderman Morris."

A great change came over the policeman. He knew now that the quiet man before him was President of the Board of Aldermen, and he began to be alarmed, remembering with what rudeness he had treated him.

"I beg your pardon, sir," he said humbly. "I didn't know you."

"What is your name, sir?" demanded the alderman, in a tone of authority.

"Jones, sir."

"How long have you been on the force?"

"Six months, your honor."

"Then you ought to be better fitted for your position by this time."

I hope you won't take no offense at what I said, not knowing you, alderman."

"That's no personal offense, but I object to your pronouncing upon the guilt of parties arrested when you know nothing of the matter."

"Shall I take the boy along, sir?"

"Yes, and this man also. I don't wish to interfere with the exercise of justice, but it is my opinion that the boy is innocent."

"I protest against this outrage," said Vincent nervously. "Am I to be punished because I expose a thief?"

"Come along, sir," said the policeman. "The alderman says so."

"I appeal to the gentlemen present," said Vincent, hoping for a forcible deliverance.

"Madam," said the alderman to the lady who had been robbed, "did you see the boy take your pocketbook?"

"No, sir! I thought it was the man, till he told me it was the boy, and the money was found on the boy."

"I should think that told the story," said Vincent. "Any man here might be arrested as soon as I. Fellow citizens, is this a free country, where a man of reputation can be summarily arrested at the bidding of another? If so, I would rather live under a monarchy."

There was a murmur of approval, and some sympathy was excited.

"There will be no injustice done, sir," said the alderman. "I propose to follow up this matter myself. I will see my friend, Mr. Waterbury, and I can soon learn whether the boy's story is correct."

"He may lie, too!" said Vincent, who had very good reasons for fearing Mr. Waterbury's testimony.

"Mr. Waterbury is a gentleman of veracity," said Alderman Morris sharply. "I see you recognize the name."

"Never heard of him," said Vincent. "I suppose it is one of the boy's confederates."

"I will answer for him," said the alderman. "My boy," he said, "I hope we shall be able to prove your innocence. Be under no anxiety. Go with the officer, and I will seek out Mr. Waterbury. Officer, take care to treat him gently."

"All right, sir."

There was no fear now that Tom would be roughly treated. He had too much regard for his own interest, and his tenure of office, to disoblige a man so influential and powerful as Alderman Morris.

Notwithstanding there had been such a turn in his favor, Tom felt humiliated to feel that he was under restraint, and his cheeks burned with shame as he walked beside the officer. Vincent, upon the other side, gnashed his teeth with rage, as he thought of his unexpected detention. Just as revenge was in his grasp, he had been caught in the same trap which he had so willingly set for Tom.

"That Alderman Morris is a fool!" he said. "He isn't fit to be in office."

"Don't you say nothin' against him!" said the policeman. "It won't be best for you. He's one of our leadin' citizens, Alderman Morris is."

"He snubbed you!" sneered Vincent. "He talked to you as if you were a dog."

"No, he didn't. You'd better shut up, prisoner."

"Oh, well, if you're willing to be trampled upon, it isn't any of my business. I wouldn't stand it, alderman or no alderman. Such things wouldn't be allowed in New York, where I live."

"Oh, New York's a model city, so I've heard," retorted the policeman, in a tone of sarcasm. "We don't pretend to come up to New York."

Finding that nothing was to be gained by continuing his attacks upon the alderman, Vincent became silent, but his brain was active. He felt that Mr. Waterbury's testimony would be fatal to him. He must escape, if possible. Soon a chance came. He seized his opportunity, shook off the grasp of the officer, and darted away. Not knowing what to do with Tom, who was also under arrest, the officer paused an instant, then, leaving our hero, hastened in pursuit.

"Now's your chance to escape, boy!" said a sympathetic bystander to him.

"I don't want to escape," answered Tom. "I want my innocence proved. I shall stay where I am till the officer returns."

And he kept his word. Ten minutes later the officer came back, puffing and panting, after an unsuccessful pursuit, prepared to find Tom gone also.

"What, are you there?" he asked, staring in wonder.

"Yes," said Tom. "I don't want to escape. I shall come out right."

"I believe you will," said the officer, with a revulsion of sentiment in Tom's favor. "Just walk along beside me, and I won't take hold of you. I'm not afraid of your running away now."

CHAPTER XVIII

TOM GETS OUT OF HIS DIFFICULTY

Tom had not been long in the stationhouse when Alderman Morris, accompanied by Mr. Waterbury, entered. The latter looked at Tom with a humorous smile.

"You don't appear to get along very well without my guardianship, Tom," he said.

"No, sir," answered Tom. "The trouble is, some of my other friends can't let me alone."

"Was it in a fit of emotional insanity that you relieved the lady of her pocketbook?" asked Mr. Waterbury, bent on keeping up the joke.

"If I ever do such a thing, you may be sure it is because I am insane," answered Tom positively.

"I shall," said Mr. Waterbury seriously. "Now, where is this precious acquaintance of ours who got you into this scrape?"

"He has escaped."

"Escaped!" exclaimed the alderman hastily. "How is that?"

Here the policeman took up the story and explained that Vincent had taken advantage of his double charge to effect his escape.

"I suppose, officer," said Mr. Waterbury, "that you were unwilling to leave Tom in order to pursue him."

"I did leave him, sir, and didn't expect to find him when I got back. But there he was, waiting for me as quietly as -- anything."

"Didn't you feel tempted to escape, too, my boy?"

"Why should I, sir? I had done nothing; I had nothing to fear."

"Innocence is not always a protection, for justice is sometimes far from clear-sighted. In the present case, however, I think you will not suffer for your confidence."

Tom was not brought to trial. Mr. Waterbury's statement of what had passed on the voyage of the River Belle was held to be sufficient to establish Tom's innocence, and he was allowed to walk out with Mr. Waterbury.

"Have you anything to do this morning, Tom?" asked his friend.

"No, sir."

"Then come around and dine with me at the Burnet House. Afterward we will call upon your friends, the Watsons."

Mrs. Watson and Jennie had altered their plans and gone to a boarding house, preferring that to a hotel.

"That will be agreeable to me, sir."

The lunch was excellent, and Tom did full justice to it.

"At one time this morning, Tom, it looked as if you would dine at quite a different place," said Mr. Waterbury, when they were eating the dessert.

"Yes, sir."

"You won't think much of Cincinnati's hospitality, eh, Tom?"

"Any place would be the same, where Vincent was," returned Tom.

"Very true; he and Graham will bring discredit on any city which they adopt as a home. How long shall you remain here?"

"I should like to stay long enough to see something of the city, but I cannot afford it. I must reach California as soon as possible."

"No doubt you are right, in your circumstances. I have been inquiring for you and find that St. Joseph, in Missouri, is the usual starting-point for travelers across the plains. I find an acquaintance here in the hotel, who will start tomorrow for that place. I have mentioned you to him, and he says he shall be glad to have your company so far. Whether you keep together afterward will depend upon yourselves."

"I shall be glad to have company, sir," said Tom. Though manly and self-reliant, he realized that it was quite a serious undertaking for a boy of his age to make the trip alone. He was not sure of meeting with another friend like Mr. Waterbury, and there might be danger of falling in with another brace of worthies like Graham and Vincent.

"My friend's name is Ferguson -- a Scotchman, rather sedate, but entirely trustworthy. I will introduce you this evening."

"Thank you, sir."

After lunch they walked to Mrs. Watson's boarding house. Somewhere on Vine Street, Mr. Waterbury paused in front of a jewelry store.

"I want to step in here a minute, Tom," he said.

"Certainly, sir."

Tom remained near the door, while Mr. Waterbury went into the back part of the store where he was occupied for a few minutes with one of the proprietors. When he came back he held a small box in his hand.

"Please carry this for me, Tom," he said.

"With pleasure, sir."

They went out into the street together.

"Do you know what is in the box, Tom?" asked Mr. Waterbury.

"No, sir," answered our hero, a little surprised at the question.

"You didn't see what I was buying, then?" continued Mr. Waterbury.

"No, sir. I was watching the crowds on the sidewalk."

"If you have any curiosity, you may open the box."

Previously Tom had felt no curiosity. Now he did feel a little.

Opening the box, his eye rested on a neat silver watch, with a chain attached. The case was a pretty one, and Tom glanced at it with approval.

"It is very pretty, sir," he said, "but I thought you had a watch already."

"I didn't buy it for myself."

"For your son?" asked Tom innocently.

Mr. Waterbury smiled.

"I thought of asking your acceptance of it," he said.

"You don't mean that you are going to give it to me, sir?" said Tom eagerly.

"If you will accept it."

"How kind you are, Mr. Waterbury!" exclaimed Tom gratefully. "There is nothing in the world that I should like so much. How can I thank you?"

"By considering it a proof of my interest in you. I was sure you would like it. Before I had reached your age the great object of my ambition was a watch. I received one from my uncle, as a gift, on my seventeenth birthday. I believe I looked at it once every five minutes on an average during the first day."

"I dare say it will be so with me, sir," said Tom, who, at the moment, had the watch in his hand, examining it.

"As you are to rough it, I thought it best to get you a hunting case watch, because it will be less liable to injury. When you become a man I hope you will be prosperous enough to buy a gold watch and chain, if you prefer them. While you are a boy silver will be good enough."

"Gold wouldn't correspond very well with my circumstances," said Tom. "I didn't dream of even having a silver watch and chain for years to come. I shall write home this evening, and tell mother of my good luck."

83

"Will you mention that you have already been under arrest?" asked Mr. Waterbury, smiling.

Tom shook his head.

"I am not proud of that," he answered, "and it would only trouble them at home to have an account of it. When I get home, I may mention it sometime."

"Better put on your watch and chain, Tom, before we reach Mrs. Watson's."

Tom needed no second invitation.

"It's lucky mother put a watch pocket in my vest," he said. "We didn't either of us suppose there would be any occasion for it, but I asked her to do it."

In a nice-looking brick boarding house -- for brown-stone houses were not then often to be found -- Tom and his friend found Mrs. Watson and Jennie.

"I'm so glad to see you, Tom," said Jennie. "I've missed you awfully."

"Thank you," said Tom. "I've come to bid you goodbye."

"Goodbye! You don't mean that?"

"I expect to start for St. Joseph tomorrow. I am in a hurry to get to California."

"That's real mean. I don't see why you can't stay in Cincinnati a week."

"I should like to."

"Then why don't you?" persisted the young girl.

"Jennie," said her mother, "we must remember that Thomas is not traveling for pleasure. He is going to California to seek his fortune. It won't do for him to linger on his way."

"A week won't make much difference; will it, Tom?"

"I am afraid it will, Jennie. Besides, a friend of Mr. Waterbury will start tomorrow, and he has agreed to take me with him."

"I suppose you've got to go, then," said Jennie regretfully. "Oh, where did you get that watch, Tom?"

"A kind friend gave it to me."

"Who do you mean -- Mr. Graham?" she asked archly.

"He would be more likely to relieve me of it. No, it is Mr. Waterbury."

"I am going to kiss you for that, Mr. Waterbury," said Jennie impulsively, and she suited the action to the word.

"What will Mr. Waterbury think, Jennie?" said her mother.

"He thinks himself well repaid for his gift," answered that gentleman, smiling, "and half inclined to give Tom another watch."

"Isn't it my turn, now?" asked Tom, with a courage at which he afterward rather wondered, but he was fast getting rid of his country bashfulness.

"I never kiss boys," said Jennie demurely.

"Then I will grow into a man as fast as I can," said Tom, "and give somebody a watch, and then -- But that will be a good while to wait."

"I may kiss you goodbye," said Jennie, "if I feel like it."

She did feel like it, and Tom received the kiss.

"It strikes me, Tom," said Mr. Waterbury, as they were walking home, "that you and Jennie are getting along fast."

"She kissed you first," said Tom, blushing.

"But the kiss she gave me was wholly on your account."

"She seems just like a sister," said Tom. "She's a tip-top girl."

CHAPTER XIX

A MISSOURI TAVERN

The next day Tom started on his way. His new companion, Donald Ferguson, was a sedate Scotchman and a thoroughly reliable man. He was possessed to the full of the frugality characteristic of the race to which he belonged, and, being more accustomed to traveling than Tom, saved our hero something in the matter of expense. He was always ready to talk of Scotland, which he evidently thought the finest country in the world. He admitted that Glasgow was not as large a city as London, but that it was more attractive. As for New York, that city bore no comparison to the chief city of Scotland.

"You must go to Scotland some time, Tom," he said. "If you can't visit but one country in the Old World, go to Scotland."

Privately Tom was of opinion that he should prefer to visit England, but he did not venture to hurt the feelings of his fellow-traveler by saying so.

"I wonder, Mr. Ferguson," he could not help saying one day, "that you should have been willing to leave Scotland, since you so much prefer it to America."

"I'll tell you, my lad," answered the Scotchman. "I would rather live in Scotland than anywhere else on God's footstool, but I won't be denying that it is a poor place for a man to make money, if compared with a new country like this."

Mr. Donald Ferguson

"There are no gold mines, I suppose, sir?"

"No, and the land is not as rich as the land here. It is rich in historical associations, but a man, you know, can't live on those," he added shrewdly.

"No, I should think not," said Tom. "It would be a pretty dry diet. How long have you been in the country, Mr. Ferguson?"

"A matter of three months only, my lad. It's the gold mines that brought me over. I read of them in the papers at home, and I took the first ship across the Atlantic."

"Have you a family, Mr. Ferguson?"

"I've got an old mother at home, my lad, who looks to me for support. I left fifty pounds with her when I came away. It'll last her, I'm thinkin', till I can send her some from California."

"Then Mr. Ferguson, you are like me," said Tom. "I am going to California to work for my father and mother. Father is poor, and I have brothers and sisters at home to provide for. I hope I shall succeed, for their sake."

"You will, my lad," said the Scotchman, in a tone of calm confidence. "It is a noble purpose, and if you keep to it God will bless you in your undertaking, and give you a good fortune."

"I hope we shall both be fortunate."

"I have no fear. I put my trust in the Lord, who is always ready to help those who are working for him."

Tom found that Mr. Ferguson, though his manner was dry and unattractive, was a religious man, and he respected and esteemed him for his excellent traits. He was not a man to inspire warm affection, but no one could fail to respect him. He felt that he was fortunate in having such a man for his companion, and he was glad that Mr. Ferguson appeared to like him in turn.

He also found that the Scotchman, though a man of peace and very much averse to quarreling, was by no means deficient in the trait of personal courage.

One evening they arrived at a small tavern in a Missouri town. Neither Tom nor his companion particularly liked the appearance of the place nor its frequenters, but it appeared to be the only place of entertainment in the settlement.

The barroom, which was the only public room set apart for the use of the guests, was the resort of a party of drunken roisterers, who were playing poker in the corner and betting on the game. At the elbow of each player was set a glass of whisky, and the end of each game was marked by a fresh glass all around.

Tom and Mr. Ferguson took a walk after supper and then sat down quietly at a little distance from the card-players, attracting at first but little attention from them.

Presently, at the close of a game, glasses were ordered for the party, at the expense of those who had suffered defeat.

"What'll you have, strangers?" inquired a tipsy fellow, with an Indian complexion and long black hair, staggering toward Ferguson.

"Thank you, sir," said the Scotchman, "but I don't drink."

"Don't drink!" exclaimed the former, in evident surprise. "What sort of a man, pray, may you be?"

"I am a temperance man," said Ferguson, adding indiscreetly, "and it would be well for you all if you would shun the vile liquor which is destroying soul and body."

"—your impudence!" cried the other, in a rage. "Do you dare to insult gentlemen like us?"

"I never insult anybody," said the Scotchman calmly. "What I have said is for your good, and you would admit it if you were sober."

"Do you dare to say I'm drunk?" demanded the man, in a fury.

"Mr. Ferguson," said Tom, in a low voice, "I wouldn't provoke him if I were you."

But the Scotchman was no coward, and, though generally prudent, he was too fond of argument to yield the point.

"Of course, you're drunk," he said calmly. "If you will reflect, you show all the signs of a man that has taken too much liquor. Your face is flushed, your hand is unsteady, and -- "

He was interrupted by a volley of execrations from the man whom he was coolly describing, and the latter, in a fit of fury, struck the Scotchman in the face. Had the blow been well directed it would, for the time, have marred the small share of personal beauty with which nature had endowed Mr. Ferguson, but it glanced aside and just struck him on his prominent cheekbone.

"A ring! A ring!" shouted the men in the corner, jumping to their feet in excitement. "Let Jim and the Scotchman fight it out."

"Gentlemen," said Mr. Ferguson, "I don't wish to fight with your friend. He is drunk, as you can see plainly enough. I don't wish to fight with a drunken man."

"Who says I am drunk?" demanded the champion of whisky. "Let me get at him."

But his friends were now holding him back. They wanted to see a square fight, according to rule. It would prove, in their opinion, a pleasant little excitement.

"I meant no offense," said Ferguson. "I only told the truth."

"You are a -- liar!" exclaimed the man, known as Jim.

"I do not heed the words of a man in your condition," said the Scotchman calmly.

"Pull his nose, Jim! Make him fight!" exclaimed the friends of the bully. "We'll back you!"

The hint was taken. Jim staggered forward, and, seizing the Scotchman's prominent nose, gave it a violent tweak.

Now there are few men, with or without self-respect, who can calmly submit to an insult like this. Certainly Mr. Donald Ferguson was not one of them. The color mantled his high cheekbones, and anger gained dominion over him. He sprang to his feet, grasped the bully in his strong arms, dashed him backward upon the floor of the barroom, and, turning to the companions of the fallen man, he said, "Now come on, if you want to fight. I'll take you one by one, and fight the whole of you, if you like."

Instead of being angry, they applauded his pluck. They cared little for the fate of their champion but were impressed by the evident strength of the stranger.

"Stranger," said one of them, "you've proved that you're a man of honor. We thought you were a coward. It's a pity you don't drink. What may your name be?"

"Donald Ferguson."

"Then, boys, here's to the health of Mr. Ferguson. He's a bully boy, and no coward."

"Gentlemen," said the Scotchman, "it's a compliment you mean, no doubt, and I'm suitably thankful. If you'll allow me, I'll drink your health in a liquor which will not injure any one. I'll wish you health and prosperity in a glass of cold water, if the barkeeper happens to have any of that beverage handy. Tom, join with me in the toast."

Tom did so, and the speech was well received.

"As for this gentleman," said Mr. Ferguson, addressing Jim, who had struggled to his feet and was surveying the scene in rather a bewildered way, "I hope he won't harbor malice; I've only got even with him. We may as well forgive and forget."

"That's the talk! Jim, drink the stranger's health!"

Jim looked a little doubtful, but when a glass of whisky was put into his hand he could not resist the seductive draft and tossed it down.

"Now shake hands!" said one of the players.

"With all my heart," said Ferguson, and the two shook hands, to the great delight of the company.

"You got off pretty well, Mr. Ferguson," said Tom, when they retired for the night.

"Yes, my lad, better than I expected. I thought once I would have to fight the whole pack. Poor fellows! I pity them. They are but slaves to their appetites. I hope, my lad, you'll never yield to a like temptation."

"No fear for me, Mr. Ferguson. I feel as you do on the subject."

The journey continued till one day, about noon, they reached the town of St. Joseph, popularly called St. Joe.

CHAPTER XX

ST. JOE

St. Joe was at that time the fitting-out point for overland parties bound for California. As a matter of course it presented a busy, bustling appearance, and it seemed full of life and movement. There was a large transient population, of a very miscellaneous character. It included the thrifty, industrious emigrant, prepared to work hard and live poorly, till the hoped-for competence was attained. But there was also the shiftless adventurer, whose chief object was to live without work, and the unscrupulous swindler, who was ready, if opportunity offered, to appropriate the hard earnings of others.

"It's a lively place, Mr. Ferguson," said Tom.

"It is, indeed, my young friend," said the cautious Scot, "but it is a place, to my thinking, where it behooves a man to look well to his purse."

"No doubt you are right, Mr. Ferguson. I have learned to be cautious since my adventure with Graham and Vincent."

"There's many like them in the world, Tom. They are like lions, going about seeking whom they may devour."

St. Joseph could not at that time boast any first-class hotels. Inns and lodging houses it had in plenty. At one of these -- a two-story building, dignified by the title of "The Pacific Hotel" -- our hero and his Scotch friend found accommodations. They were charged two dollars and a half per day -- the same price they charged at first-class hotels in New York and Boston, while their rooms and fare were very far from luxurious. The landlord was a stout, jolly host, with a round, good-natured face.

"You and your son will room together, I suppose," he said.

"He isn't my son, but a young friend of mine," said Mr. Ferguson.

"I thought he didn't look much like you," said the landlord.

"I am hard and weather-beaten, while he is young and fresh."

"Well, gentlemen, I wish you both good luck. What will you take? I have a superior article of whisky that I can recommend."

"Thank you, but I beg you will excuse me, sir," said Ferguson. "I never drink."

"Nor I," said Tom, "but I am much obliged to you all the same."

"Well, that beats me," said the landlord. "Why, you don't know what's good. You ain't a minister, are you?" turning to Ferguson.

"I have not that high distinction, my friend. I am an unworthy member of the church of Scotland."

"I don't think your countrymen generally refuse whisky."

"So much the worse for them. They are only too fond of it. My own brother died a miserable death, brought on by his love of liquor."

"Then I won't press you, but I say, strangers, you won't find many of your way of thinking in the country you're going to."

"I don't doubt he's right, Tom," said Ferguson to Tom, as they entered the chamber assigned to them. "We may not be together always. I hope you won't be led away by them who offer you strong drink. It would be the ruin of you, boy."

"Don't fear for me, Mr. Ferguson. I have no taste for it."

"Sometimes it's hard to refuse."

"It won't be hard for me."

"I am glad to hear you say that, my lad. You are young, strong, and industrious. You'll succeed, I'll warrant, if you steer clear of that quicksand."

Later in the day the two friends began to make inquiries about overland travel. They had no wish to remain long at St. Joe. Both were impatient to reach the land of gold, and neither cared to incur the expense of living at the hotel any longer than was absolutely necessary. Luckily this probably would not be long, for nearly every day a caravan set out on the long journey, and doubtless they would be able to join on agreeing to pay their share of the expenses. It was a great undertaking, for the distance to be traversed was over two thousand miles, through an unsettled country, some of it a desert, with the chances of an attack by hostile Indians, and the certainty of weeks, and perhaps months, of privation and fatigue. Mr. Donald Ferguson looked forward to it with some apprehension, for, with characteristic Scotch caution, he counted the cost of whatever he undertook and did not fail to set before his mind all the contingencies and dangers attending it.

"It's a long journey we're going on, my lad," he said, "and we may not reach the end of it in safety."

"It isn't best to worry about that, Mr. Ferguson," said Tom cheerfully.

"You are right, my lad. It's not for the best to worry, but it is well to make provision for what may happen. Now, if anything happens to me, I am minded to make you my executor."

"But don't you think I am too young, Mr. Ferguson?"

"You are o'er young, I grant, but you are a lad of good parts, temperate, steady and honest. I have no other friend I feel like trusting."

"I hope, Mr. Ferguson, there will be no occasion to render you any such service, but whatever I can I will do."

"It will be very simple. You will take my money, and see that it is sent to my mother, in Glasgow. I will give you her address now, and then, if any sudden fate overtakes me, there will be no trouble. You will know just what to do."

Tom was flattered by this mark of confidence. It was evident that the cautious Scotchman had formed a very favorable opinion of him, or he would not have selected so young a boy for so important a trust.

"Will you do the same for me, Mr. Ferguson?" he asked, with the sudden reflection that, young as he was, there was no absolute certainty of his living to reach California.

"Surely I will, my lad."

"If I should die I should want any money I might have left sent to my father."

"Give me his address, my lad, and it shall be done. It is a good precaution, and we shan't either of us die the sooner for doing our duty, to the best of our ability, by those who would mourn our loss."

Tom and his friend instituted inquiries, and ascertained that two days later a caravan was to start on its way across the continent. They ascertained, also, that the leader of the expedition was a pioneer named Fletcher, who was making his home at the California Hotel. They made their way thither and were fortunate enough to find Mr. Fletcher at home. He was a stout, broad-shouldered man and a practical farmer, who was emigrating from Illinois. Unlike the majority of emigrants, he had his family with him, namely, a wife, and four children, the oldest a boy of twelve.

"My friend," said Ferguson, "I hear that you are soon leaving here with a party for California."

"I leave day after tomorrow," answered Fletcher.

"Is your party wholly made up?"

"We are about full, but we might receive one or two more."

"My young friend and I wish to join some good party, as we cannot afford to remain here, and we are anxious to get to work as soon as possible."

Some care needed to be exercised in the choice of a party, as there were some who would only give trouble and annoyance, or perhaps fail to pay their proper share of the expenses. But Ferguson's appearance was sufficient guarantee of his reliability, and no one was likely to object to Tom.

"Of course," added Ferguson, "we are ready to bear our share of the expense."

"Then you can come," said Fletcher. "You will both need revolvers, for we may be attacked by Indians and must be able to defend ourselves."

"Certainly, we will do our part, if need be."

This was an expense which Tom had not foreseen, but he at once saw the importance of being armed when crossing such a country as lay before them, and he went with Ferguson to make the needful purchase. His Scotch friend instructed him in the method of using his new weapon, and Tom felt a boy's natural pride in his new acquisition. He felt years older then he did on the morning when he left his country home. He had gained some knowledge of the world and felt a greater confidence in himself on that account. He looked forward to the remainder of his journey with pleasurable excitement and lost no time in making the necessary preparations.

CHAPTER XXI

HOW THINGS WENT ON AT HOME

While Tom was slowly making his way westward, there was one place where tidings from him were anxiously awaited and where nightly prayers were offered for his health and safe progress. Of course this was the dear, though humble, farmhouse, which had been his home.

Twice a week Tom wrote, and his letters were cheerful and reassuring.

"Don't trouble yourself about me, dear mother," he wrote from Cincinnati. "I am making friends and learning how to travel. I feel years older and rely much more on myself than when, an inexperienced boy, I bade you goodbye. I am a thousand miles from you, and the longest and most difficult part of the journey lies before me, but with health and strength, and prudence, I hope to arrive in good condition at my destination. As to health I never felt better in my life, and I have taken lessons in prudence and caution which will be of essential service to me. I have found that a boy who goes out into the world to seek his fortune cannot trust everybody he falls in with. He will find foes as well as friends, and he will need to be on his guard.

"I start tomorrow for St. Joseph, in Missouri, going by way of St. Louis. Mr. Donald Ferguson, a middle-aged Scotchman, is my companion. A younger and livelier companion might prove more agreeable, but perhaps not so safe. Mr. Ferguson is old enough to be my father, and I shall be guided by his judgment where my own is at fault. He is very frugal, as I believe his countrymen generally are, and that, of course, just suits me. I don't know how long I shall be in reaching St. Joseph, but I shall write you once or twice on the way. Give my love to father, Sarah, Walter, and Harry, and keep a great deal for yourself.

"Your loving son,

"Tom."

"Tom is growing manly, Mary," said Mark Nelson to his wife. "It's doing him good to see a little of the world."

"I suppose it is, Mark," said his wife, "but the more I think of it the more I feel that he is very young to undertake such a long journey alone."

"He is young, but it will make a man of him."

"He must be having a tip-top time," said Walter. "I wish I were with him."

"You would be more of a hindrance than a help to him, Walter," said Mark Nelson.

"You are only a child, you know," said Sarah, in an elder-sister tone.

"What do you call yourself?" retorted Walter. "You are only two years older than I am."

"Girls always know more than boys of the same age," said Sarah condescendingly. "Besides, I haven't said anything about going out to California."

"No, I should think not. A girl that's afraid of a mouse had better stay at home."

Walter referred to an incident of the day previous, when the sudden appearance of a mouse threw Sarah into a panic.

"Are there any mouses in California?" asked little Harry, with interest.

"If there are I could carry a cat with me," returned Sarah good-humoredly.

Mark Nelson, though he felt Tom was a boy to be trusted, did ask himself occasionally whether he had been wise in permitting him to leave home under the circumstances. Suppose he continued in health, there were doubts of his success. His golden dreams might not be realized. The two hundred dollars which he had raised for Tom might be lost and bring in no return, and this would prove a serious loss to Mark, hampered as he was already by a heavy mortgage on his farm. Would Squire Hudson be forbearing, if ill-luck came? This was a question he could not answer. He only knew that such was not the squire's reputation.

"Well, Mr. Nelson, what do you hear from Tom," asked the squire, one day about this time. "How far is he on his way?"

"We received a letter from Cincinnati yesterday. He then was about starting for St. Joseph."

"Does he seem to enjoy the journey?"

"He writes in excellent spirits. He says he has met with good friends."

"Indeed! How does his money hold out?"

"He does not speak of that."

"Oh, well, I dare say he is getting along well," and the squire walked on.

"Does he feel interested in Tom, or not?" queried Mark Nelson, as he looked thoughtfully after the squire, as he walked on with stately steps, leaning slightly on his gold-headed cane. He might have been enlightened on this point, if he could have heard a conversation, later in the day, between Squire Hudson and his son Sinclair.

"I saw Mark Nelson this morning," he observed at the supper table.

"Has he heard from Tom?"

"Yes. His son wrote him from Cincinnati."

"I wish I could go to Cincinnati," grumbled Sinclair. "I think I have a better right to see the world than Tom Nelson."

"All in good time, my son. Tom is not traveling for pleasure."

"Still, he is getting the pleasure."

"He will have to work hard when he reaches California. Probably he won't have a cent left when he gets there."

"What will he do then?"

"He must earn money."

"Do you think he will do well, father?"

"He may, and then again he may not," answered the squire judicially.

"If he don't, how is he going to pay you back the money you lent him?"

"I always thought your father was foolish to lend his money to a boy like that," said Mrs. Hudson querulously.

"Women know nothing about business," said the squire, with an air of superior wisdom.

"Sometimes men don't know much," retorted his wife.

"If you refer to me, Mrs. Hudson," said her husband, "you need have no anxiety. I did not lend the money to the boy, but to his father."

"That isn't much better. Everybody knows that Mark Nelson has all that he can do to get along. His wife hasn't had a new dress for years."

The squire's face grew hard and stern. He had never loved his wife, and never forgiven Mrs. Nelson, whom he had loved as much as he was capable of doing, for refusing his hand.

"She has made her bed, and she must lie upon it," he said curtly. "She might have known that Mark Nelson would never be able to provide for her."

"Perhaps she never had any other offer," said Mrs. Hudson, who was ignorant of a certain passage of her husband's life.

"Probably she did, for she was a very pretty girl."

"Then she's faded," said Mrs. Hudson, tossing her head.

Squire Hudson did not reply, but as his eyes rested on the sharp, querulous face of his helpmate, and he compared it mentally with the pleasant face of Mrs. Nelson, he said to himself that, faded or not, the latter was still better looking than his wife had been in the days of her youth. Of course it would not do to say so, for Mrs. Hudson was not amiable.

"Mark Nelson has given me security," said the squire, returning to the point under discussion. "I hold a mortgage on his farm for the whole amount he owes me."

"Do you think you shall have to foreclose, father?" asked Sinclair.

"If Tom does not succeed in California, I probably shall," said the squire.

"Do you think he will succeed?"

"He may be able to make a living, but I don't think he will be able to help his father any."

"Then why did you lend him the money?"

"He wanted to go and was willing to take the risk. I lent the money as a business operation."

"Suppose Mr. Nelson loses his farm, what will he do?" inquired Sinclair.

"I really don't know," answered the squire, shrugging his shoulders. "That is no concern of mine."

"Tom wouldn't put on so many airs if his father had to go to the poorhouse," said Sinclair.

"Does he put on airs?"

"He seems to think he is as good as I am," said Squire Hudson's heir.

"That is perfectly ridiculous," said Mrs. Hudson. "The boy must be a fool."

"He is no fool," said the squire, who did not allow prejudice to carry him so far as his wife and son. "He is a boy of very fair abilities, but I apprehend he will find it harder to make his fortune than he anticipated. However, time will show."

"Most likely he'll come home in rags and grow up a day-laborer," said Sinclair complacently. "When I'm a rich man I'll give him work. He won't feel like putting on airs, then."

"What a good heart Sinclair has!" said Mrs. Hudson admiringly.

Squire Hudson said nothing. Possibly the goodness of his son's heart was not so manifest to him.

CHAPTER XXII

THE YOUNG MAN FROM BOSTON

Soon after leaving St. Joe, the emigrant train which Tom had joined entered the territory of Kansas. At that early day the settlement of this now prosperous State had scarcely begun. Its rich soil was as yet unvexed by the plow and the spade, and the tall prairie grass and virgin forest stretched for many and many a mile westward in undisturbed loneliness.

One afternoon, toward the setting of the sun, the caravan halted on the site of the present capital of the state, Topeka. The patient oxen, wearied with the twenty miles they had traveled, were permitted to graze. The ten baggage wagons or "ships of the plain," as they were sometimes called, came to anchor in a sea of verdure. They were ranged in a circle, the interior space being occupied as a camping ground. Then began preparations for supper. Some of the party were sent for water. A fire was built, and the travelers, with a luxurious enjoyment of rest, sank upon the grass.

**The caravan stops to rest. ("Nooning on the Platte"
by Albert Bierstadt)**

Donald Ferguson looked thoughtfully over the vast expanse of unsettled prairie, and said to Tom, "It's a great country, Tom. There seems no end to it."

"That's the way I felt when I was plodding along today through the mud," said Tom, laughing.

"It's because the soil is so rich," said the Scotchman. "It'll be a great farming country some day, I'm thinking."

"I suppose the soil isn't so rich in Scotland, Mr. Ferguson?"

"No, my lad. It's rocky and barren and covered with dry heather, but it produces rare men, for all that."

Mr. Ferguson was patriotic to the backbone. He would not claim for Scotland what she could not fairly claim, but he was all ready with some compensating claim.

"How do you stand the walking, Mr. Ferguson?"

"I'm getting used to it."

"Then it's more than I am. I think it's beastly."

These words were not uttered by Tom, but by rather a dandified-looking young man, who came up limping. He was from Boston and gave his name as Lawrence Peabody. He had always lived in Boston, where he had been employed in various genteel avocations, but in an evil hour he had been lured from his comfortable home by the seductive cry of gold and, laying down his yardstick, had set out for California across the plains. He was a slender young man, with limbs better fitted for dancing than for tramping across the prairie, and he felt bitterly the fatigue of the journey.

"Are you tired, Mr. Peabody?" asked Tom.

"I am just about dead. I didn't bargain for walking all the way across the prairies. Why couldn't old Fletcher let me ride?"

"The oxen have had all they could do today to draw the wagons through the mud."

"Look at those boots," said the Bostonian ruefully, pointing to a pair of light calfskin boots, which were so overlaid with mud that it was hard to tell what was their original color. "I bought those boots in Boston only two weeks ago. Everybody called them stylish. Now they are absolutely disreputable."

"It seems to me, my friend," said the Scotchman, "that you did not show much sagacity in selecting such boots for your journey. My young friend, Tom, is much better provided."

"His boots are cowhide," said Mr. Lawrence Peabody disdainfully. "Do you think I would wear cowhide boots?"

"You would find them more serviceable, Mr. Peabody," said Tom. "Besides, I don't believe anybody could tell the difference now."

"How much did you pay for them?" asked the Bostonian.

"A dollar and a half."

"Humph! I thought so," returned Peabody contemptuously. "We don't wear cowhide boots in Boston."

"You are not in Boston now."

"I wish I was," said Peabody energetically. "I wouldn't have started if I had known what was before me. I expected to travel like a gentleman, instead of wading through this cursed mud till I'm ready to drop. Look at my pantaloons, all splashed with mire. What would my friends say if I should appear in this rig on Washington Street?"

"They might take you for a bogtrotter," said Tom, smiling.

"I have always been particular about my appearance," said Peabody plaintively. "'He looks just as if he'd come out of a bandbox,' some of my lady friends used to say. How do I look now?"

"Like a dirty-handed son of toil," said Tom humorously.

"So do you," retorted Peabody, who felt that this was uncomplimentary.

"I admit it," said Tom, "and that's just what I expect to be. You don't expect to dig gold with kid gloves on, do you, Mr. Peabody?"

"I wish I had brought some with me," said the Bostonian seriously. "It would have saved my hands looking so dingy."

Mining for gold was not easy work. Here, a miner sifts for gold on the American River in California, 1850.

"How came you to start for California, my friend?" inquired Ferguson.

"The fact is," said Peabody, "I am not rich. There are members of our family who are wealthy, but I am not one of the lucky number."

"You were making a living at home, were you not?"

"Yes, but my income was only enough for myself."

"I suppose you were in love, then," said Tom.

"I don't mind saying that I was, confidentially, of course," said Mr. Peabody complacently.

"Was your love returned?"

"I may say it was. The young lady was the daughter of a merchant prince. I saw that she loved me, but her father would not consent to our union, on account of my limited means. I read in the Transcript of the gold discoveries in California. I determined to go out there and try my fortune. If I am successful I will go home and, with a bag of gold in each hand, demand the hand of Matilda from her haughty sire. When he asks me for my credentials, I will point to the gold and say, 'Behold them here!'"

"If both your hands are full I don't see how you can point to the bags of gold," said Tom, who liked to tease the young Bostonian.

"There are a great many things you don't understand," said Mr. Peabody, irritably.

"He is right, Tom," said Ferguson, with a quiet smile.

"If you are both against me, I will give it up," said Tom. "All I can say is, I hope you'll get the two bags of gold, Mr. Peabody, and that you'll get the young lady, too."

Here Fletcher came up, and called upon Tom to assist in preparations for supper. Our hero readily complied with the request. Indeed, he always showed himself so obliging that he won the favorable regards of all.

Mr. Peabody continued the conversation with Mr. Ferguson.

"Do you think there's as much gold in California as people say?" he asked.

"No," answered the Scotchman.

"You don't?" exclaimed the Bostonian, in dismay.

"No. People always magnify when they talk of a new country. Now, my friend, how much do you expect to get in the first year?"

"Well, about fifty thousand dollars," answered Peabody.

"And how much were you earning in Boston -- a thousand dollars?"

"About that," answered Peabody vaguely. In fact, he had been working on a salary of twelve dollars a week in a retail dry-goods store on Washington Street.

"Then you expect to make fifty times as much as at home?"

"Don't you think I will?"

"I have never had such large expectations. If I make three or four thousand dollars in twelve months it will satisfy me."

"But a man would never get rich, at that rate," said Lawrence Peabody uneasily.

"I don't know about that. It depends as much on what a man does with his money, as on the amount he makes," said the prudent Scot.

"I am afraid I did wrong in leaving Boston," said Peabody gloomily. "If I am to travel many weeks through the mud and get no more than that, I shall feel that I am poorly paid."

"You don't feel like my young friend Tom. He is full of hope and enjoys everything."

"He hasn't been brought up as I have," said Peabody. "A country boy in cowhide boots is tough and don't mind roughing it."

Ferguson did not have a chance to answer, for there was a summons to supper -- a welcome call that made even Mr. Lawrence Peabody look cheerful for the time being.

CHAPTER XXIII

MR. PEABODY'S TROUBLES

When the party camped for the night the custom was to arrange the baggage wagons in a semicircle, and provide a resting place for the women and children inside. As they were passing through a country occupied by Indians it was necessary to post one or more sentinels to keep watch through the night and give notice of any who might be seen lurking near the camp. Fortunately, however, an Indian attack was seldom made at night. The time generally selected was in the morning, when the party were preparing to start on their day's march. Tom, as a boy, would have been excused taking his turn, but this did not suit him. He requested as a favor that he might stand watch with the rest.

"Can he be relied upon? Is he not too young?" asked Fletcher, the leader, of Mr. Ferguson.

"You can depend upon him," said the Scotchman confidently. "There's more manliness in Tom than in many men of twice his years."

"Then I will put his name on the list," said Fletcher.

"That's right. I'll answer for him."

But there was one of the travelers who was by no means eager to stand on watch. This was Lawrence Peabody, the young man from Boston. He sought an interview with Fletcher and asked to be excused.

"On what grounds, Mr. Peabody?" asked Fletcher, surprised.

"It doesn't agree with me to lose my night's sleep," said Peabody. "I am naturally delicate, and --"

"Your excuse is not satisfactory, Mr. Peabody. We are banded together in a little community, having mutual rights and mutual obligations. In the arrangements made for the common safety it is your duty to bear your part."

"I am willing to provide a substitute," said Peabody eagerly.

"Where will you find a substitute?"

"I have been talking with Tom Nelson. He says he is willing to serve in my turn."

"He will serve when his own turn comes; that will be all we can expect of him."

"But he is only a boy. Why should he be expected to take his turn?"

"If he is old enough to be a substitute, he is old enough to stand watch for himself."

"But, Mr. Fletcher, I am very delicate," protested Lawrence Peabody. "I must have my regular sleep, or I shall be sick."

"We must take our chances of that, Mr. Peabody."

"I shall be very likely to go to sleep on my post."

"I wouldn't advise you to," said Fletcher seriously. "It might be dangerous."

"Dangerous!" cried Peabody nervously.

"Precisely. If a lurking Indian should surprise you, you might wake up to find yourself scalped."

"Good gracious!" exclaimed the Bostonian, his teeth chattering, for he was not of the stuff of which heroes are made. "Do you … think there is any danger of that?"

"Considerable, if you neglect your duty."

"But perhaps I can't help falling asleep."

"Mr. Peabody," said Fletcher sternly, "you must keep awake. Not only your own safety, but that of the whole camp, may depend upon your vigilance. If you choose to risk your own life, I don't complain of that, but you shall not imperil ours. I therefore give you notice, that if you fall asleep on guard you will be drummed out of camp and left to shift for yourself."

"But I couldn't find my way on the prairie," said Peabody, very much alarmed.

"You had better think of that when you are tempted to close your eyes, Mr. Peabody," replied Fletcher.

Lawrence Peabody walked off, feeling very much disconcerted. Fervently he wished himself back in Boston, where there are no Indians and a man might sleep from one week's end to another without any danger of losing his scalp.

"What's the matter, Mr. Peabody?" asked Tom, observing his melancholy appearance.

"I don't think I shall ever live to see California," answered Mr. Peabody plaintively.

"Why, what's the matter now?" asked Tom, checking an inclination to laugh. "Are you sick?"

"I don't feel very well, Tom. I'm very delicate, and this journey is almost too much for my strength."

"Oh, cheer up, Mr. Peabody! Think of the gold that awaits you at the end of the journey."

"It's all that keeps me up, I do assure you. But I am afraid I shall never live to get there," said Peabody, with a groan.

"Don't think of such things, Mr. Peabody. Of course none of us is sure of living, but the chances are that we shall reach California in health, make our fortunes, and go home rich. At any rate, that's what I am looking forward to."

"I wouldn't mind so much but for one thing, Tom."

"What is that?"

"Fletcher insists that I shall take my turn in standing guard. If I were not so delicate I wouldn't mind, but I know I can't stand it. I'll give you two dollars to take my place, every time my turn comes."

"I am willing, if Mr. Fletcher is," said Tom, who was by no means averse to making a little extra money.

"But he isn't. I proposed it to him, for I was sure I could arrange with you, but he refused."

"I suppose," said Tom slyly, "he thought I couldn't fill your place. You are a brave, resolute man, and I am only a boy."

"Tom -- I -- I don't mind telling you, but I am afraid I am not brave."

"Oh, nonsense, Mr. Peabody! That is only your modesty."

"But I assure you," said the young Bostonian earnestly, "I am speaking the truth. If I should see an Indian crawling near the camp I'm really afraid I should faint."

"You won't know how brave you are till you are put to the test."

"But do you think there is any chance of my being put to the test? Do you think there are any Indians near?" asked Lawrence Peabody, wiping the damp perspiration from his brow.

"Of course there must be," said Tom. "We are passing through their hunting grounds, you know."

"Why did I ever leave Boston?" said Mr. Peabody sadly.

"You came, as I did, to make your fortune, Mr. Peabody."

"I'm afraid I can't keep awake, Tom. Mr. Fletcher tells me, if I don't, that he will turn me adrift on the prairie. Isn't that hard?"

"I am afraid it is a necessary regulation. But you won't fall asleep. Your turn will only come about once in two weeks, and that isn't much."

"The nights will seem very long."

"I don't think so. I think it'll be fun, for my part."

107

"But suppose -- when you are watching -- you should all at once see an Indian, Tom?" said Peabody, with a shiver.

"I think it would be rather unlucky for the Indian," said Tom coolly.

"You are a strange boy, Tom," said Mr. Peabody.

"What makes you think so?"

"You don't seem to care anything about the danger of being scalped."

"I don't believe I should like being scalped any more than you do."

"You might have got off from standing watch, but you asked to be allowed to."

"That is quite true, Mr. Peabody. I want to meet my fair share of danger and fatigue."

"You can stand it, for you are strong and tough. You have not my delicacy of constitution."

"Perhaps that's it," said Tom laughing.

"Would you mind speaking to Fletcher and telling him you are willing to take my place?"

"I will do it, if you wish me to, Mr. Peabody."

"Thank you, Tom. You are a true friend," and Mr. Peabody wrung the hand of his young companion.

Tom was as good as his word. He spoke to Fletcher on the subject, but the leader of the expedition was obdurate.

"Can't consent, my boy," he said. "It is enough for you to take your turn. That young dandy from Boston needs some discipline to make a man of him. He will never do anything in a country like California unless he has more grit than he shows at present. I shall do him a favor by not excusing him."

Tom reported the answer to Peabody, who groaned in spirit, and nervously waited for the night when he was to stand watch.

CHAPTER XXIV

A SAD SIGHT

A day later, while the wagon train was slowly winding through a mountain defile, they encountered a sight which made even the stout-hearted leader look grave. Stretched out stiff and stark were two figures, cold in death. They were men of middle age, apparently. From each the scalp had been removed, thus betraying that the murderers were Indians.

"I should like to come across the red devils who did this," said Fletcher.

"What would you do with them?" asked Ferguson.

"Shoot them down like dogs, or if I could take them captive they should dangle upon the boughs of yonder tree."

"I hope I shall be ready to die when my time comes," said Ferguson, "but I want it to be in a Christian bed and not at the hands of a dirty savage."

Just then Lawrence Peabody came up. He had been lagging in the rear, as usual.

"What have you found?" he inquired, not seeing the bodies at first, on account of the party surrounding them.

"Come here, and see for yourself, Peabody," said one of the company.

Lawrence Peabody peered at the dead men -- he was rather nearsighted -- and turned very pale.

"Is it the Indians?" he faltered.

"Yes, it's those devils. You can tell their work when you see it. Don't you see that they are scalped?"

"I believe I shall faint," said Peabody, his face becoming of a greenish hue. "Tom, let me lean on your shoulder. Do -- do you think it has been done lately?"

"Yesterday, probably," said Ferguson. "The bodies look fresh."

"Then the Indians that did it must be near here?"

"Probably."

"These men were either traveling by themselves or had strayed away from their party," said Fletcher. "It shows how necessary it is for us to keep together. In union there is strength."

The bodies were examined. In the pocket of one was found a letter addressed to James Collins, dated at some town in Maine. The writer appeared to be his wife. She spoke of longing for the time when he should return with money enough to redeem their farm from a heavy mortgage.

"Poor woman!" said Ferguson. "She will wait for her husband in vain. The mortgage will never be paid through his exertions."

Tom looked sober, as he glanced compassionately at the poor emigrant.

"He came on the same errand that I did," he said. "I hope my journey will have a happier ending."

"Always hope for the best, Tom," said his Scotch friend. "You will live happier while you do live, and, if the worst comes, it will be time enough to submit to it when you must."

"That is good philosophy, Mr. Ferguson."

"Indeed it is, my lad. Don't borrow trouble."

"We must bury these poor men," said Fletcher. "We can't leave them out here, possibly to be devoured by wild beasts. Who will volunteer for the service?"

"Come, Peabody," said John Miles, a broad-shouldered giant, who had a good-natured contempt for the young man from Boston. "Suppose you and I volunteer."

Lawrence Peabody shrank back in dismay at the unwelcome proposition.

"I couldn't do it," he said shivering. "I never touched a dead body in my life. I am so delicate that I couldn't do it, I assure you."

"It's lucky we are not all delicate," said Miles, "or the poor fellows would be left unburied. I suppose if anything happens to you, Peabody, you will expect us to bury you?"

"Oh, don't mention such a thing, Mr. Miles," entreated Peabody, showing symptoms of becoming hysterical. "I really can't bear it."

"It's my belief that nature has made a mistake, and Peabody was meant for a woman," said Miles, shrugging his shoulders.

"I will assist you, my friend," said the Scotchman. "It's all that remains for us to do for the poor fellows."

"Not quite all," said Tom. "Somebody ought to write to the poor wife. We have her address in the letter you took from the pocket."

"Well thought of, my lad," said Fletcher. "Will you undertake it?"

"If you think I can do it properly," said Tom modestly.

"It'll be grievous news, whoever writes it. You can do it as well as another."

In due time Mrs. Collins received a letter revealing the sad fate of her husband, accompanied with a few simple words of sympathy.

Over the grave a rude cross was planted, fashioned of two boards, with the name of James Collins, cut out with a jack-knife, upon them. This inscription was the work of Miles.

"Somebody may see it who knows Collins," he said.

It happened that, on the second night after the discovery of Collins and his unfortunate companion, Lawrence Peabody's turn came to stand watch. He was very uneasy and nervous through the day. In the hope of escaping the ordeal he so much dreaded he bound a handkerchief round his head.

"What's the matter, Mr. Peabody?" asked Fletcher.

"I've got a fearful headache," groaned Peabody. "It seems to me as if it would split open."

"Let me feel of it," said Fletcher. "It doesn't feel hot. It doesn't throb," he said.

"It aches terribly," said Peabody. "I'm very subject to headaches. It is the effect of a delicate constitution."

"The fellow is shamming," said Fletcher to himself, and he felt disgust rather than sympathy.

"It's a little curious, Mr. Peabody, that this headache should not come upon you till the day you are to stand on watch," remarked the leader, with a sarcasm which even the young man from Boston detected.

"Yes, it's strange," he admitted, "and very unlucky, for of course you won't expect a sick man to watch."

"You don't look at it in the right light, Mr. Peabody. I regard it as rather lucky than otherwise."

Lawrence Peabody stared.

"I don't understand you, Mr. Fletcher," he said.

"If you have the headache, it will prevent you from going to sleep, and you remember you expressed yourself as afraid that you might. If you were quite well, I might feel rather afraid of leaving the camp in your charge. Now, I am sure you won't fall asleep."

Mr. Peabody listened in dismay. The very plan to which he had resorted in the hope of evading duty was likely to fasten that duty upon him.

"He'll be well before night," thought Fletcher shrewdly, and he privately imparted the joke to the rest of the party. The result was that Mr. Peabody became an object of general attention.

In half an hour the young man from Boston removed his handkerchief from his head.

"Are you feeling better, Mr. Peabody?" asked Tom.

"Very much better," said Peabody.

"Your headache seems to pass off suddenly."

"Yes, it always does," said the young Bostonian. "I am like mother in that. She had a delicate constitution, just like mine. One minute she would have a headache as if her head would split open, and half an hour afterward she would feel as well as usual."

"You are very fortunate. I was afraid your headache would make it uncomfortable for you to watch tonight."

"Yes, it would, but, as the captain said, it would have kept me awake. Now I don't believe I can keep from sleeping on my post."

"Why don't you tell Fletcher so?"

"Won't you tell him, Tom? He might pay more attention to it if you told him."

"No, Mr. Peabody. You are certainly the most suitable person to speak to him. What makes you think he would pay more attention to me, who am only a boy?"

"He seems to like you, Tom."

"I hope he does, but really, Mr. Peabody, you must attend to your own business."

Fletcher was at the head of the train, walking beside the first wagon. Hearing hurried steps, he turned, and saw Mr. Lawrence Peabody, panting for breath.

"Have you got over your headache, Mr. Peabody?" he asked, with a quiet smile.

"Yes, Mr. Fletcher, it's all gone."

"I am glad to hear it."

"It would have kept me awake tonight, as you remarked," said Peabody. "Now, I am really afraid that I shall fall asleep."

"That would be bad for you."

"Why so?"

"You remember those two poor fellows whom we found scalped the other day?"

"I shall never forget them," said Lawrence Peabody, with a shudder.

"Better think of them tonight. If you go to sleep on watch, those very Indians may serve you in the same way."

"Oh, good gracious!" cried Peabody, turning pale.

"They or some of their tribe are, no doubt, near at hand."

"Don't you think you could excuse me, Mr. Fletcher?" stammered Peabody, panic-stricken.

"No!" thundered Fletcher, so sternly that the unhappy Bostonian shrank back in dismay.

For the credit of Boston, it may be said that John Miles -- a broad-shouldered young giant, who did not know what fear was -- more honorably represented the same city.

CHAPTER XXV

A NIGHT PANIC

Lawrence Peabody's feelings when night approached were not unlike those of a prisoner under sentence of death. He was timid, nervous and gifted with a lively imagination. His fears were heightened by the sad spectacle that he had recently witnessed. His depression was apparent to all, but I regret to say that it inspired more amusement than sympathy. Men winked at each other as they saw him pass, and, with the exception of Tom and his Scotch friend, probably nobody pitied the poor fellow.

"He's a poor creature, Tom," said Donald Ferguson, "but I pity him. We wouldn't mind watching tonight, but I doubt it's a terrible thing to him."

"I would volunteer in his place, but Mr. Fletcher won't agree to it," said Tom.

"He is right. The young man must take his turn. He won't dread it so much a second time."

"What would the poor fellow do if he should see an Indian?"

"Faint, likely, but that is not probable."

"Mr. Fletcher thinks there are some not far off."

"They don't attack in the night, so I hear."

"That seems strange to me. I should think the night would be most favorable for them."

"It's their way. Perhaps they have some superstition that hinders."

"I am glad of it, at any rate. I can sleep with greater comfort."

The rest were not as considerate as Tom and Ferguson. They tried, indeed, to excite still further the fears of the young Bostonian.

"Peabody," said Miles, "have you made your will?"

"No," answered Peabody nervously. "Why should I?"

"Oh, I was thinking that if anything happened to you tonight you might like to say how your things are to be disposed of. You've got a gold watch, haven't you?"

"Yes," said Peabody nervously.

"And a little money, I suppose."

"Not very much, Mr. Miles."

"No matter about that. Of course if you are killed you won't have occasion for it," said Miles, in a matter-of-fact tone.

"I wish you wouldn't talk that way," said Peabody irritably. "It makes me nervous."

"What's the use of being nervous? It won't do any good."

"Do you really think, Mr. Miles, there is much danger?" faltered Peabody.

"Of course there is danger. But the post of danger is the post of honor. Now, Peabody, I want to give you a piece of advice. If you spy one of those red devils crouching in the grass, don't stop to parley, but up with your revolver, and let him have it in the head. If you can't hit him in the head, hit him where you can."

"Wouldn't it be better," suggested Peabody, in a tremulous voice, "to wake you up, or Mr. Fletcher?"

"While you were doing it the savage would make mincemeat of you. No, Peabody, fire at once. This would wake us all up, and if you didn't kill the reptile we would do it for you."

"Perhaps he would see me first," suggested Peabody, in a troubled tone.

"You mustn't let him. You must have your eyes all about you. You are not near-sighted, are you?"

"I believe I am -- a little," said Peabody eagerly, thinking that this might be esteemed a disqualification for the position he dreaded.

"Oh, well, I guess it won't make any difference, only you will need to be more vigilant."

"I wish I was blind, just for tonight," thought Peabody to himself, with an inward sigh. "Then they would have to excuse me."

John Miles overtook Fletcher, who was with the head wagon.

"Captain Fletcher," he said, "I am afraid Peabody will make a mighty poor watch."

"Just my opinion."

"He is more timid than the average woman. I've got a sister at home who has ten times his courage. If she hadn't I wouldn't own the relationship."

"I am not willing to excuse him."

"Of course not, but I'll tell you what I'll do. I'll keep an eye open myself, so that we sha'n't wholly depend on him."

"If you are willing to do it, Miles, we shall all be indebted to you. Don't let him know it, though."

"I don't mean to. He shall suppose he is the only man awake in camp."

At a comparatively early hour the party stretched themselves out upon the ground, inviting sleep. Generally they did not have to wait long. The day's march brought with it considerable physical fatigue. Even those who were light sleepers at home slept well on the trip across the plains. Few or none remained awake half an hour after lying down. So Peabody knew that he would soon be practically alone.

With a heavy heart he began to pace slowly forward and back. He came to where Tom lay.

"Tom -- Tom Nelson," he called, in a low voice.

"What's the matter?" asked Tom, in a sleepy tone.

"Are you asleep?"

"No, but I soon shall be."

"Won't you try to keep awake a little while? It won't seem so lonesome."

"Sorry I can't accommodate you, Mr. Peabody, but I'm awfully tired and sleepy."

"Who's that talking there?" drowsily demanded the nearest emigrant. "Can't you keep quiet, and let a fellow sleep?"

"Good night, Mr. Peabody," said Tom, by way of putting an end to the conversation.

"Good night," returned the sentinel disconsolately.

The hours passed on, and Lawrence Peabody maintained his watch. He was in no danger of going to sleep, feeling too timid and nervous. He began to feel a little more comfortable. He could see nothing suspicious and hear nothing except the deep breathing of his sleeping comrades.

"It is not so bad as I expected," he muttered to himself.

He began to feel a little self-complacent and to reflect that he had underrated his own courage. He privately reflected that he was doing as well as any of his predecessors in duty. He began to think that after he had got back to Boston with a fortune, gained in California, he could impress his friends with a narrative of his night-watch on the distant prairies. But his courage had not yet been tested.

He took out his watch to see how time was passing.

It pointed to twelve o'clock.

Why there should be anything more alarming in twelve o'clock than in any other hour I can't pretend to say, but the fact none will question. Mr. Peabody felt a nervous thrill when his eyes rested on the dial. He looked about him, and the darkness seemed blacker and more awe-inspiring than ever, now that he knew it to be midnight.

"Will it ever be morning?" he groaned. "Four long hours at least before there will be light. I don't know how I am going to stand it."

Now, there was attached to the wagon-train one of those universally despised but useful animals, a donkey, the private property of a man from Iowa, who expected to make it of service in California. The animal was tethered near the camp and was generally quiet. But tonight he was wakeful, and managed about midnight to slip his tether, and wandered off. Peabody did not observe his escape. His vigilance was somewhat relaxed, and with his head down he gave way to mournful reflection. Suddenly the donkey, who was now but a few rods distant, uplifted his voice in a roar which the night stillness made louder than usual. It was too much for the overwrought nerves of the sentinel. He gave a shriek of terror, fired wildly in the air, and sank fainting to the ground. Of course the camp was roused. Men jumped to their feet, and, rubbing their eyes, gazed around them in bewilderment.

It was not long before the truth dawned upon them. There lay the sentinel, insensible from fright, his discharged weapon at his feet. The almost equally terrified donkey was in active flight, making the air vocal with his peculiar cries.

There was a great shout of laughter, in the midst of which Peabody recovered consciousness.

"Where am I?" he asked, looking about him wildly, and he instinctively felt for his scalp, which he was relieved to find still in its place.

"What's the matter?" asked the leader. "What made you fire?"

"I -- I thought it was the Indians," faltered Peabody. "I thought I heard their horrid war-whoop."

"Not very complimentary to the Indians to compare them with donkeys," said Miles.

Lawrence Peabody was excused from duty for the remainder of the night, his place being taken by Miles and Tom in turn.

It was a long time before he heard the last of his ridiculous panic, but he was not sensitive as to his reputation for courage, and he bore it, on the whole, pretty well.

CHAPTER XXVI

MR. PEABODY IS WORSTED

The traveler of today who is whirled across the continent in six days and a half has little conception of what the overland journey was in the year 1850. Week after week and month after month slipped away between the start and the arrival on the western slope of the Sierra Nevadas. Delicate women and children of tender years developed extraordinary endurance and showed remarkable fortitude on the wearisome trip. But the hope of bettering their fortunes was the magnet that drew them steadily on, day after day, in their march across the plains.

The travelers are looking forward to searching for gold. Pictured here are miners in the Sierra Nevada Mountains in 1852.

Tom was at an age when adventure has a charm. His feet were often weary, but he never tired of the journey. Every morning found him active, alert, and ready for the toilsome walk. He was, indeed, impatient for the time to come when he could be earning something to pay up his debt to Squire Hudson, and so relieve his father from the additional burden assumed for his sake. Otherwise he was quite content to plod on, seeing something new every day.

"You're always cheerful, Tom, my lad," said Ferguson one day.

"Yes," said Tom. "I am having a good time."

"Youth is aye the time for enjoyment. When I was a lad like you I might have been the same."

"Don't you enjoy the journey, Mr. Ferguson?" asked Tom.

"I'm getting tired of it, Tom. I look upon it as a means to an end. I'm in a hurry to reach the mines."

"So am I, Mr. Ferguson, for that matter."

"And I can't help thinking, what if they don't turn out as well as we expect? Then there'll be months lost, besides a good bit of money," replied Ferguson.

"Oh, I'm sure there is plenty of gold, and we shall get our share," said Tom confidently. "That is, if we have our health."

"I hope it'll be as you say, my lad. Indeed, I think you are right. You have taught me a lesson."

"Have I, Mr. Ferguson? What is it?"

"Always to look on the bright side. It is a lesson worth learning. It makes a man feel happier and often gives courage to press on to the accomplishment of his purpose."

"I suppose it is natural to me," said Tom.

"It is a happy gift. It is a pity that poor creature from Boston hadn't it."

Lawrence Peabody was approaching, and this no doubt led to the allusion. He was limping along, looking decidedly down in the mouth, which, indeed, was not unusual.

"What is the matter with you, Mr. Peabody?" asked Tom.

"I'm almost gone," groaned Peabody. "My strength is exhausted, and, besides, I've got a terrible corn on my left foot."

"How long has that been?"

"For two or three days. It's torture for me to walk. I don't know but you'll have to leave me here on the prairie to perish."

"Not so bad as that, Mr. Peabody, I hope. Perhaps Mr. Chapman will lend you his donkey to ride upon."

The owner of the donkey was within hearing distance, and at once expressed a willingness to lend his animal to Mr. Peabody.

"That will be better than perishing on the prairies," said Tom cheerfully.

"I am not much used to riding," said Peabody cautiously.

"He won't run away with you, Peabody," said the owner. "He's too lazy."

Lawrence Peabody was already aware of this fact, and it gave him courage to accept the offered help. He mounted Solomon -- as the donkey was called, for some unknown reason -- and for a time enjoyed the relief from the toil of walking. He became quite cheerful and was disposed to congratulate himself upon his success, when an unfortunate fit of obstinacy came over Solomon. It dawned upon the sagacious animal that it would be much easier to travel without a load, and, turning his head, he looked thoughtfully at his rider.

"Get up, Solomon!" exclaimed Peabody, striking the animal on the haunch.

Solomon felt that this was taking a personal liberty and he stood stock-still, his face expressive of obstinacy.

"Why don't he go on?" asked Peabody, perplexed.

"He's stopping to rest," said Tom. "I am afraid he is lazy."

"Go along!" exclaimed Peabody, again using his whip. But the animal did not budge.

"This is really very provoking," murmured the rider. "What shall I do?"

"Don't give up to him," advised one of the company. "Here, let me whip him."

"Thank you. I wish you would."

It was an unlucky speech. The other complied with the request and delivered his blow with such emphasis that Solomon's equanimity was seriously disturbed. He dashed forward with what speed he could command, Mr. Peabody holding on, in a sort of panic, till he was a hundred yards away. Then he stopped suddenly, lowering his head, and his hapless rider was thrown over it, landing some distance in advance. Solomon looked at him with grim humor, if a donkey is capable of such a feeling and, apparently satisfied, turned and walked complacently back to the wagon-train.

Several of the company, witnessing the accident, hurried forward to Mr. Peabody's assistance. They picked him up, groaning and bewildered, but not much hurt.

"None of your limbs broken," said Miles. "I guess you'll do."

"I'm badly shaken up," moaned Peabody.

"It will do you good," said Miles bluntly.

"You had better try it yourself, then," retorted Peabody, with unwonted spirit.

"Good for you!" laughed Miles. "I suspect you are not dead yet."

"What made you put me on such a vicious beast?" asked Peabody of the owner.

"Solomon isn't vicious; he's only lazy," said Chapman. "We can't blame him much."

"I think he ought to be shot," said Peabody, painfully rising and stretching out one limb after another to make sure that none was broken.

"You seem to be unlucky, Mr. Peabody," said Tom.

"I'm always unlucky," moaned Peabody.

"Will you ride again, Mr. Peabody?" asked Chapman. "I'll catch Solomon for you, if you like."

"Not for fifty dollars!" exclaimed Peabody energetically. "It is as much as anybody's life is worth."

"If you will make me the same offer, I won't refuse, Mr. Chapman," said Tom.

"You can mount him, if you like."

Tom waited for no second invitation. He approached Solomon cautiously, vaulted upon his back, and the animal, disagreeably surprised, had recourse to the same tactics which had proved so successful in the case of the young man from Boston. But he had a different kind of a rider to deal with. Tom had been accustomed to ride from the time he was six years of age, and he stuck to his seat in spite of all attempts to dislodge him. So far from feeling alarmed, he enjoyed the struggle.

"It's no go, Solomon!" he said gaily. "You've tackled the wrong customer this time. Better make up your mind to go as I want you to."

Solomon came to the same conclusion after a time. He had tried his ordinary tactics, and they had proved unavailing. The struggle had been witnessed with some interest by the other members of the company.

"You can ride, youngster; that's a fact," said the owner of the donkey. "I didn't say anything, but I rather expected to see you follow Peabody."

"I'm used to riding," said Tom modestly. "Mr. Peabody is not."

"Every lad ought to know how to ride," said Ferguson. "It's a deal manlier than smoking a cigar, to my thinking."

"I can smoke a cigar," said Peabody, desirous probably of appearing to possess one manly accomplishment.

"You will hardly find it as useful as riding in the new country you are going to, Mr. Peabody," said Ferguson dryly.

"I'd give something for a good cigar myself," said John Miles.

121

"I prefer riding," said Tom. "I never smoked a cigar in my life."

"You are just as well off without it, my lad," said the Scotchman. "It don't do men any good, and always harms boys."

Peabody never again mounted Solomon. One trial was sufficient, and, footsore and lame as he was, he decidedly preferred to walk.

CHAPTER XXVII

THE LOST HORSE

Day followed day, and every sunset found the party from eighteen to twenty miles nearer the land of gold. They had not yet been molested by Indians, though on more than one occasion they had encountered the remains of those whom the savages had ruthlessly slaughtered. When they witnessed such a spectacle they were moved less by fear than indignation.

"I didn't think I should ever thirst for a fellow creature's blood," said John Miles, "but if I could meet the savages that did this bloody work, I would shoot them down like dogs and sleep all the more soundly for it. How is it with you, friend Ferguson?"

"I am inclined to agree with you," said the Scotchman. "When an Indian makes himself a beast of prey he should be treated accordingly."

"Are there any Indians in California?" asked Peabody nervously.

"I don't think we shall have any trouble with them there, Mr. Peabody," said Ferguson.

"Then I wish I was there now. It must be terrible to be scalped," and the young man from Boston shuddered.

"I don't think it would be an agreeable surgical operation," said Fletcher, who had just come up. "Let us hope that we shall not be called upon to undergo it."

The next morning, when breakfast was over and the party was preparing to start, an unpleasant discovery was made. One of the most valuable horses was missing. He must have slipped his tether during the night and strayed away. As they were situated, the loss of such an animal would be felt.

"He can't be far away," said Fletcher. "Some of us must go after him."

"Let Peabody mount the mustang and undertake to find him," suggested John Miles, winking at the captain.

"Mr. Peabody," said Captain Fletcher gravely, "will you undertake to recover the horse? We shall all feel under great obligations to you."

"I -- I hope you will excuse me, Captain Fletcher," stammered Peabody in great alarm. "I know I couldn't find the horse. I shouldn't know where to look."

"This is where he got away. You can see his trail in the grass," said Scott, a young man from Indiana. "All you will have to do will be to follow the trail, Mr. Peabody."

"I'm very nearsighted," pleaded Peabody. "I should lose my way, and never come back."

"Carrying the mustang with you? That would be a loss indeed," said John Miles pointedly. "On the whole, Captain Fletcher, we had better excuse Mr. Peabody."

"Mr. Peabody is excused," said the leader.

"Thank you," said Peabody, looking relieved. "I would go, I am sure, if I could do any good, but I know I couldn't."

"Who will volunteer?" asked Fletcher.

"Let me go," said Tom eagerly.

"You are not afraid of losing your way, Tom?" said Miles.

"No, or if I do, I will find it again."

"That boy is more of a man now than Peabody will ever be," said Miles, in a low voice to Ferguson.

"That he is," said the Scotchman, who was a firm friend of our young hero. "There is the making of a noble man in him."

"I believe you."

"I have no objection to your going, Tom," said Fletcher, "but it is better that you should have company. Who will go with the boy?"

"I," said several, among them John Miles and Henry Scott.

"You may go, Scott," said the leader. "I have work for Miles at camp. The sooner you get started the better."

"All right, captain. Come along, Tom."

The two were in the saddle before two minutes had passed and, guided by the trail, struck out upon the prairie.

Scott was a tall, broad-shouldered young farmer, not over twenty-five, strong and athletic, and reported, the best runner, wrestler, and vaulter in the party. Tom was very well pleased to have his company.

CHAPTER XXVIII

INDIAN CASUISTRY

"I should like to know when the horse got away," said Scott, as he and Tom rode on side by side, "then we could calculate how far we should have to go before overtaking him."

"He wouldn't be likely to travel all the time, would he?" asked Tom.

"Probably not. He may have gone only a mile or two. Are your eyes good?"

"Pretty good."

"Look about, then, and see if you can anywhere see anything of the rover."

Scott and Tom, drawing rein, looked searchingly in all directions, but nowhere was the lost animal visible.

"Somebody may have found him," suggested Tom.

"That may be. If so, we have a harder job before us."

The prairie was not quite level but was what is called a rolling prairie, and this limited the view. Otherwise it would have been easy for a person, whose sight was keen, to have distinguished an object as large as a horse at a distance of many miles.

"Are you sure we are on the right track, Mr. Scott?" asked Tom.

"Yes, I can see by the trail."

"I can see no hoof-marks."

"Not just here, but look closely, and you will see slight marks of disturbance in the grass. As long as these signs last we need have no doubts as to our being on the right track."

"The same trail will lead us back to our party," said Tom.

"Yes, I shouldn't like to part from them in this country. It would be rather a bad place to be lost without provisions."

They had ridden about five miles when the trail became clearer and better defined. In fact, the marks in the prairie grass appeared more numerous than a single horse would be likely to make.

Scott looked grave.

"We will halt here a moment, Tom," he said. "I want to examine the trail."

"Shall I get off my horse?"

"No, it is not necessary."

Scott dismounted and walked about, closely examining the marks in the grass.

Finally he looked up.

"I begin to think it doubtful whether we shall recover Dan," he said.

"Why?"

"He has been found and carried off," was the reply. "Do you see the double trail?"

"Yes," said Tom, after a brief examination.

"It means that a horseman has found Dan and led him away. This rather complicates matters."

"What do you think we had better do?" inquired Tom.

"That requires consideration. I could tell better if I knew by whom the horse had been found. The finder may be honest and would, in that case, surrender it on our appearing and claiming him. But, again, he may be dishonest, and resist our claims."

"We are two to one," said Tom stoutly.

"We don't know that. The man may belong to a party."

"The members of his party would know that the horse was not his."

"Quite true, if the party was composed of decent persons, like our own, but that is not certain."

"Then will you go back without Dan?" asked Tom.

"I don't want to do that. In fact I should be ashamed to. Captain Fletcher would conclude that he might as well have sent Peabody, and I am not anxious to be classed with him."

"Nor I," said Tom, smiling.

"So the only thing is to push on, and make what discoveries we may."

"All right," said Tom cheerfully.

They rode on for a couple of miles, having no difficulty in following the trail, until they reached the brow of a small eminence. Here they were greeted with a sight that startled them. A group of a dozen Indians were reclining on the grass, with their horses fastened near them. Startled as they were, they detected the animal of which they were in search among the Indian horses.

"We've walked into a trap with our eyes open, Tom," said Scott, halting his horse mechanically. His bronzed face was a little pale, for he knew well the character of the savages before him, the hopelessness of escape, and the terrible fate that probably awaited them.

"Shall we turn and fly, Mr. Scott?" asked Tom hurriedly.

"It would be of no use, Tom. We must stay and face the music."

Upon the appearance of the two friends the Indians had sprung to their feet, and the colloquy was scarcely over before there was an Indian at each bridle-rein. They made signs, easily understood, for Tom and Scott to dismount.

"Stop a minute," said Scott, with creditable coolness, considering the great peril in which he knew himself to be. "Is there any one here who speaks English?"

An elderly Indian stepped forward quickly and said, "Speak, white man. I speak English a little."

"Good," said Scott. "Then I want you to tell your friends here that I came after a horse that left our camp last night. Do you understand?"

The Indian inclined his head.

"There he is," continued Scott, pointing with his finger to Dan. "Give him to me, and I will go away."

The interpreter turned to his companions and repeated what Scott had said. Evidently it was not favorably received, as Scott could see by the menacing looks that were turned upon him. He waited, with some anxiety, for the answer to his claim. He had to wait for some minutes, during which the Indians appeared to be consulting. It came at last.

"The white man has lied," said the Indian sententiously. "The horse is ours."

"That's pretty cool, eh, Tom?" said Scott, provoked not only by the denial of his claim, but by the charge of falsehood.

Tom did not answer, thinking silence more prudent.

The Indian interpreter looked suspiciously from one to the other. He understood what "cool" meant, but was not familiar with the special sense in which Scott used it.

"I will prove that the horse is ours," said Scott. "Here, Dan!"

The horse whinnied and tried to reach Scott, upon hearing his name pronounced.

"There," said Scott triumphantly, "you see the horse knows me. I have not lied."

The speech was an imprudent one. Indians are not lawyers, but they understand the familiar saying that "possession is nine points of the law." That the horse was a valuable one they understood, and they had no intention of parting with him. Still more, they looked with covetous eyes at the horses ridden by Scott and the boy, and they had already made up their minds to seize them also.

"The white man is a magician," said the interpreter. "He has bewitched the horse. The horse is ours. He has always belonged to us."

"It's no use, Tom," said Scott. "They are bound to keep Dan, and I don't see how we can help it. We had better give him up and get away if we can. All the same, the fellow is an outrageous liar."

He spoke in a low voice, and the interpreter, though listening attentively, did not quite catch what was said.

"I guess you are right," said Tom.

Scott turned to the interpreter.

"Well, if you think it is yours, squire, I reckon you will keep it. So we'll say good morning and go."

He pulled the rein, but the Indian at his bridle did not let go.

"Good morning, gentlemen," said Scott. "We are going."

"White man must stay," said the Indian interpreter decisively.

"Why?" demanded Scott impatiently.

"He has tried to steal Indian's horse," said the wily savage.

"Well, by gosh, that's turning the tables with a vengeance," cried Scott. "They're rather ahead of white rogues, Tom. Will you let the boy go?" he asked.

"White boy stay, too," answered the interpreter, after a brief reference to the leader of the Indian party.

"Tom," said Scott rapidly and not appearing to be excited, lest his excitement should lead to suspicion, "none of them are mounted. Lash your horse, and tear from the grasp of the man that holds him. Then follow me. It is our only chance."

Tom's heart beat rapidly. He knew that all his nerve was called for, but he did not falter.

"Give the signal," he said.

"One, two, three!" said Scott rapidly. Simultaneously both lashed their horses. The startled animals sprang forward. The grips of the Indians, who were not suspecting any attempts at escape, were already relaxed, and before they were fully aware of what was intended our two friends were galloping away.

CHAPTER XXIX

A RACE FOR LIFE

The Indians were taken by surprise. They so outnumbered their intended captives that they had not anticipated an attempt at escape. But they had no intention of losing their prey. There was a howl of surprise and disappointment. Then they sprang for their horses and, with little delay, were on the track of our two friends.

The delay was small, but it was improved by Scott and Tom. Pressing their animals to their highest speed they gained a lead of several hundred feet before their savage pursuers had fairly started. It was well that Tom was a good rider, or he might not have been able to keep his seat. In fact, he had never ridden so rapidly before, but he felt that he was riding for his life and was only anxious to ride faster. Scott had felt a little anxious on this point, but his anxiety vanished when he saw how easily and fearlessly his boy companion kept at his side.

"Well done, Tom!" he said as they flew over the prairie. "Keep up this pace, and we will escape yet."

"I can do it, if my horse holds out," returned Tom briefly.

Scott looked over his shoulder, and, brave man as he was, it almost made him shudder. The whole party of Indians was on his track. He could see their dusky faces, distorted by wrath, and the longing for a vicious revenge. He knew that Tom and he had little to hope for if they were caught. Fortunately their horses were strong and fleet, and not likely to break down.

"Ride for your life, Tom!" he shouted. "They will show us no mercy if they catch us."

"All right, Mr. Scott!" said Tom, his face flushed and panting with excitement. If he had not felt that so much depended upon it; if he could have thrust out from his mind the sense of the awful peril in which he stood, he would have enjoyed the furious pace at which his horse was carrying him.

The horses ridden by the Indians were not equal in speed or endurance to those which the two friends bestrode. They were fresher indeed, but they did not make up for the difference between them. There was one exception, however: Dan, the stolen horse, was not only equal to either of their horses but had the advantage of being fresher. This, after a while, began to tell. It was ridden by a young Indian brave, a brother of the leader. Soon he drew away from his companions and, yard by yard, lessened the distance between himself and the pursued. At the end of three miles he was close upon them, and at least fifty rods in advance of his comrades. Scott saw this in one of his backward glances.

"Tom," said he, "the redskin on Dan is overhauling us."

"Will he catch us?"

"I mean to catch him," said Scott coolly.

Tom did not need to ask for an explanation. Scott wheeled round, took hasty but accurate aim at the Indian, and fired. The hapless warrior reeled in his saddle, loosed his hold of the reins, and fell to the ground, while his horse, continuing in his course, his pace accelerated by fright, soon galloped alongside of Scott. There was a howl of rage from the main body of Indians, who saw the fate of their comrade without being able to help him.

"Now, Tom, ride as you never rode before!" shouted Scott. "We will circumvent those Indian devils yet and bring Dan safe into camp. Come along, Dan, old fellow. You're doing nobly."

Dan recognized the familiar voice. He entered into the spirit of the race and, relieved from the weight of his rider, dashed forward with increased speed till he led, and Scott and Tom were forced to follow.

The Indians were mad with rage. Their comrade had received a fatal wound. They saw the round hole in his breast, from which the life-blood was gushing, and they thirsted for vengeance.

Should two palefaces, one of them a boy, escape from them? That would be a disgrace, indeed. The blood of their brother called for blood in return.

Could they have inspired their horses with the same spirit which animated themselves, they might, perhaps, have overtaken their intended captives, but, happily for our two friends, the horses were less interested than their riders.

The danger was well-nigh over. It was scarcely two miles to the camp. There they would be so reinforced that the Indians would not venture an attack. That was the goal they had in view. Already they could see in the distance the wagon-train, ready for a start. They were surely safe now. But at this unlucky moment Tom's horse stumbled. The motion was so rapid that he could not retain his seat. He was thrown over the horse's head, and lay stunned and insensible upon the ground. His horse kept on his way to the camp.

CHAPTER XXX

TOM BECOMES AN INDIAN

Scott did not immediately notice Tom's mishap. The boy had shown himself so good a rider that such an accident had not occurred to him as likely to happen. When he did look back there was already a considerable distance between them. In fact, Tom lay midway between the Indians and himself.

What was he to do?

If he returned there was no hope of rescuing Tom, and he would infallibly fall into the hands of the Indian pursuers. In that case his fate was sealed. He had killed an Indian warrior, and his life would pay the forfeit. By going on he could head a rescuing party from the camp. His heart ached for Tom. It was hard to leave him in the hands of the savage foe; but Tom was a boy, and there was hope that he would be spared. So, he felt that it was better to continue his flight.

There was a shout of fierce joy when the Indians saw Tom's fall. They would have preferred to capture Scott, for he it was who had killed their comrade, but they were glad to have one prisoner. They reined up their horses and halted beside the still insensible boy. They held a brief consultation and decided not to continue the pursuit. They could see the encampment, which Scott was sure to reach before he could be overtaken. They could not tell the number of the party to which he belonged, but, being few in numbers themselves, the risk would be a hazardous one. They decided to retire with their prisoner. Tom was lifted to a seat in front of one of the party, and they rode leisurely back.

This was the position in which our hero found himself when he roused from his stupor. One glance revealed to him the whole. His heart sank within him. They might kill him. Remembering the ghastly sights he had seen on his trip across the plains, he thought it likely that they would. Life was sweet to Tom. To what boy of sixteen is it not? It seemed hard to be cut off in the threshold of an active career, and to but cut off by savage hands. But there was an additional pang in the thought that now he would be unable to help his father. The result of his plan would only be to impose an additional burden upon the modest home which his father found it so hard to keep up. Tom sighed, and, for the first time in his life, he felt discouraged.

He looked about him, scanning the dark, grave faces, and read no hope or encouragement in any. Finally the Indians came to a halt at their old camping-ground, and Tom was lifted from the horse. He was placed upon the ground, in the center of the group. Then followed a consultation. From the glances directed toward him Tom understood that he was the subject of deliberation. In fact, his fate was being decided.

It was certainly a trying ordeal for our young hero. He was not sure of half an hour's life. An unfavorable decision might be followed by immediate execution. Tom felt that his best course was to remain perfectly passive. He could not understand what was said, but we are able to acquaint the reader with the general purport of the conference.

Several of the Indians favored immediate death.

"Our brother's blood calls for vengeance," they said. "The white boy must die."

"The boy did not kill him," said others. "It was the white warrior who spilled our brother's blood. He must be pursued and slain."

"What, then, shall be done with the boy? Shall he go?"

"No, we will keep him. He has strong limbs. We will adopt him into our tribe. He will make a brave warrior."

"He shall be my brother," said the chief. "I will take him in place of my brother who is dead."

There was a low murmur of approval. Even those who had first recommended the infliction of death seemed to have changed their minds. They looked at the boy as he lay stretched out upon the ground. He was stout, comely and strongly made. He had proved that he was an admirable rider. If he should join them he would grow up into a warrior who would do credit to their tribe.

So the matter was settled. The only thing that remained was to acquaint the prisoner with the decision.

The interpreter approached Tom, and said, "White boy, you are our captive. Why should we not kill you?"

"You can if you wish," answered Tom, "but why should you kill me? I have done you no harm."

"Our brother is killed. He lies dead upon the plain."

"I did not kill him," said Tom.

"The white boy speaks truth. He did not kill our brother, but his white friend took his life."

"You ought not to kill me for that," said Tom, gathering courage, for he inferred he was to live.

"The white boy speaks truth, and therefore he shall live, but he must join us. He must live with us, hunt with us, and fight for us."

"You want me to become an Indian!" cried Tom.

"We will take you in place of the warrior that is gone," said the interpreter.

Tom looked thoughtful. He did not enjoy the prospect before him, but it was, at all events, better than death. While there was life there was hope of escape. He concluded to make one appeal for freedom and, if that was denied, to accept the proposal.

"I have a father and mother far away," he said. "I have brothers and a sister, who will mourn for me. My father is poor; he needs my help. Let me go back to them."

The interpreter communicated Tom's words to his companions, but it was easy to see that they were not favorably received. The original advocates of the death penalty looked at our hero with hostile eyes, and he saw that he had made a mistake.

"The white boy must become one of us; he must take our brother's place, or he must die," said the interpreter.

Tom very sensibly concluded that it would be better to live with the Indians than to be killed and signified his acceptance of the offer. Upon this the Indians formed a circle about him and broke into a monotonous chant, accompanied with sundry movements of the limbs, which appeared to be their way of welcoming him into their tribe.

It seemed like a dream to Tom. He found it very hard to realize his position, so unexpectedly had he been placed in it. He could not help wondering what the family at home would say when they should learn that he had joined an Indian tribe far beyond the Mississippi.

CHAPTER XXXI

TOM GIVES A MAGICAL SOIREE

Tom had no intention of passing his life with the Indians. In joining them he submitted to necessity. It gave him a respite and a chance to devise plans of escape. He understood very well that, if he made the attempt and failed, his life would be the forfeit. But Tom determined to take the risk, though his life was sweet to him. Of course, he had to wait for a favorable opportunity.

There was a chance of his being rescued by his party, but this chance was diminished by the decision of his Indian captors to break camp and proceed in a northerly direction, while the course of the emigrant train was, of course, westward. Little time was wasted. The Indians mounted their horses, Tom being put on the horse of the fallen brave. The leader put himself at the head, and Tom was placed in the center, surrounded by Indians. It was evident that they were not willing to trust him yet. They meant to afford him no chance of escape.

As the only one of the band with whom Tom could converse was the interpreter, who rode at the head with the chief, he rode in silence. The Indians on either side of him never turned their heads toward him but, grave and impassive, rode on, looking straight before them.

"This is easier than walking," thought Tom, "but I would a hundred times rather walk with Scott, or Miles, than ride in my present company."

They rode for three hours, and then dismounted for the midday rest.

Nothing had been seen or heard of his old friends, and that made Tom anxious and thoughtful.

"They have gone on without me, leaving me to my fate," he said to himself, and the reflection gave him a pang. He had been on such pleasant and friendly terms with the whole party, that this cold desertion -- as it appeared -- wounded him. The young are more sensitive in such cases than their elders. As we grow older we cease to expect too much of those whose interests differ from our own.

Tom felt that his fate was more and more bound up with the Indians. If some days should pass before he could escape, he would find himself in an embarrassing condition. Suppose he got away safely, he would find himself in a pathless plain, without provisions, and with no other guide than the sun. If he should meet with no party, he would die of starvation. The prospect seemed by no means bright.

I am bound to say that, for a time, Tom, in spite of his bright, sanguine temperament, was greatly depressed. But his spirits were elastic.

"I won't give up to despair," he said to himself. "Something tells me that I shall come out right. I must wait and watch my chances."

Upon this his face brightened, and his air, which had been listless, became more animated. The Indians glanced at him, with grave approval. They concluded that he was becoming reconciled to living among them.

When the simple midday meal was placed upon the ground, and the Indians gathered around it in a sitting posture, Tom followed their example and did full justice to the meal. In fact, he had taken so much exercise that he felt hungry. Besides, he knew that he must keep up his strength, if he wished to escape. So, instead of keeping aloof in sullen dissatisfaction, he displayed a "healthy appetite."

After resting several hours the Indians resumed their journey but did not travel far. They were in no hurry. They had no long journey to make across the continent. They only wished to go far enough to be safe from attack by a rescuing party of Tom's friends. Again they encamped, and this time, from the preparations made, he understood that it was for the night.

One thing Tom could not help noticing -- the silence of these red children of the plains. They seemed to make no conversation with each other, except on necessary matters, and then their words were few in number, replies being often made in a monosyllable.

"They don't seem very social," thought Tom. "I suppose they have nothing to talk about. I wonder if the squaws ever have sewing-circles. If they have, they can't be much like Yankee women if they don't find plenty to talk about."

The silence became oppressive. Tom would have liked to take a walk, but he knew that this would not be allowed. It would be thought that he wanted to escape. Yet to sit mute hour after hour seemed to Tom intolerably stupid. A bold idea came to him. He would try to afford them some amusement.

Accordingly, he said to the interpreter, "Shall I show you a trick?"

The interpreter communicated the proposal to his comrades, and permission was granted.

Tom took from his pocket a penny. He explained to the interpreter that he would swallow the penny, and make it come out at his nose -- a common boy's trick. The Indians, to whom this also was communicated, looked curious and incredulous, and Tom proceeded.

Now, I am not going to explain how Tom accomplished the illusion. That I leave to the ingenuity of my boy readers to discover. It is enough to say that he succeeded, to the great amazement of his copper-colored spectators. There was a chorus of "Ughs!" and Tom was requested to repeat the trick.

He did so, the Indians being as puzzled as before.

Now, Indians are, in many respects, like children. They displayed, on this occasion, a childish curiosity and wonder that amused Tom. They insisted on his opening his month, to ascertain whether there was any hidden avenue from his mouth to his nose, and found, to their surprise, that his mouth was like their own. Then one of the Indians volunteered to try the experiment and nearly choked himself with the penny, which, it must be remembered, was one of the large, old-fashioned, copper coins, in circulation before the war. It cannot be said that he turned black in the face, but he certainly gasped and rolled his eyes in a manner that alarmed his friends, and they instinctively looked to Tom for help. Tom was equal to the emergency. He rose hastily, slapped the Indian forcibly on the back, and the cent was ejected from his mouth.

There was another chorus of "Ughs!" and it was evident that Tom had risen vastly in their opinion. They looked upon him as a white magician and were even a little afraid that he might work them injury in some way. But Tom's frank, good-humored manner reassured them. They asked him, through the interpreter, if he could perform any other tricks. Tom knew a few that he had learned out of an old tattered book which had fallen in his way at home; and such as he had facilities for, he attempted, to the great delight of his new friends. Tom was becoming popular, and even those who had at first recommended death were glad that his life had been spared.

CHAPTER XXXII

TOM'S ESCAPE

Night came, and the Indian camp was hushed and still. It was long before Tom went to sleep. Generally he was a good sleeper, but his mind at present was too active for slumber. "How long is this strange life going to last?" he asked himself. "How long am I to be exiled from civilization?" This was more easily asked than answered.

When he slept, his sleep was troubled. He dreamed that Lawrence Peabody was a captive, and that the chief was about to scalp him, when suddenly he awoke. He could not at first tell where he was, but a glance revealed the disheartening truth.

He must have slept several hours, for the gray dawn was creeping up the sky, heralding sunrise. He leaned on his elbow and bent a searching glance upon his companions. They were stretched motionless upon the ground, hushed in the insensibility of sleep. "Are they asleep?" Tom asked himself. He satisfied himself that the slumber was genuine, and there sprang up in his heart the wild hope of escape. A few rods distant the horses were fastened. Could he unfasten and mount one before any of them awakened?

Tom's heart beat quick with excitement. He knew that he ran a fearful risk, but he made up his mind that now was his time.

Slowly, and without noise, he raised himself to his feet. As he stood erect, he closely scanned the sleepers. There was not a motion. With stealthy steps he crept to the horses. He selected the one he had ridden the day before and unloosed him. The animal gave a slight whinny, and Tom's heart was in his throat. But no one stirred. He quickly mounted the animal and walked him for a few rods, then gave him a loose rein and was soon speeding away. Just then the sun rose, and this guided him in the direction he was to take.

He had got a mile away when, looking back through the clear air, he saw to his dismay that his flight had been discovered. The Indians were mounting their horses.

**Indians searching for "The Lost Trail"
by Karl Ferdinand, circa 1856**

"I must gallop for life," thought Tom. "They will kill me if they catch me."

He urged on his horse by all the means in his power. Luckily it was one of the two fleetest horses the Indians possessed, the other being ridden by their leader.

Tom's hope was sustained by this fact, which he had proof of the day before.

Rather to his surprise, he did not feel as much frightened as he anticipated. He felt excited, and this was his prominent feeling. Probably he felt like a soldier in the heat of battle.

But the odds against Tom were terrible, and his chance of escape seemed very slender. Behind him was a band of savages, accustomed to the plains and strong, wily, enduring, and persistent. He was new to the plains, and a mere boy. Moreover, he did not know where to find his party. There were no sign-boards upon the prairies, but a vast, uniform expanse stretching farther than the eye could reach.

Inch by inch, foot by foot, the Indians gained upon him, the leader considerably in advance.

Even if he alone were to overtake Tom, our hero would of course be no match for a strong, full-grown warrior, more especially as he had no weapon with him. By some mischance he had left it in the camp.

Tom's heart began to fail him. His horse could not always, perhaps not long, keep up his headlong speed. Then would follow capture and a painful death.

"It's hard," thought Tom sadly, "hard for me and for my dear parents and brothers and sisters. Why did I ever leave home?"

He turned in the saddle and saw the Indian leader, evidently nearer. But he saw something else. He saw a herd of buffaloes, thousands in number, impetuously rushing across the plain from the west. Their speed was great. They seemed to be blindly following their leader.

"Good heavens!" exclaimed Tom in great excitement, "the Indians are in their path. If the herd does not stop, they will be destroyed."

The Indians were fully aware of their great danger. They knew the plains well, and the terrible, resistless power of these wild herds when once on the march. They no longer thought of Tom but of their own safety. But the buffaloes were close at hand. They were sweeping on like a whirlwind. The Indians could only ride on and trust to clear them. But their pathway was wide. It reached to within a furlong of where Tom was riding. They never paused. Some of the animals in the advance might have veered to the right or left on seeing the Indians, but the pressure from behind prevented them. The savages saw their fate, and it inspired them with more dread than an encounter with white foes. Finally, they halted in despair, and their fate overtook them. Riders and steeds were overthrown as by a flash of lightning. The dark, shaggy herd did not stop, but dashed on. Tom, in awe and excitement, halted his horse, and watched the terrible sight. He could not but sympathize with his late companions, though he knew they would have taken his life.

The buffaloes passed on, but left no life behind them. The Indians and their horses were all trampled to death. Tom was alone upon the plains.

He thanked God in his heart for his self-deliverance, though he shuddered at the manner in which it was wrought. He, too, had been near being overwhelmed, but, through God's mercy, had escaped.

But for what had he escaped? Unless he found his own party, or some other, he would starve to death, or might fall into the power of some other tribe of Indians. He must ride on.

An hour later he thought he saw in the distance a solitary horseman. It might be an Indian, but that was not likely, for they generally traveled in numbers. It was more likely to be a white man. Any white man would be a friend and could guide him to safety, unless he were himself lost. At any rate, there seemed but one course to follow and that was to ride toward the stranger.

When Tom drew near his heart was filled with sudden joy, for, in the new arrival, he recognized John Miles. Miles was no less delighted.

"Tom, old boy," he said, "is it you? How did you get away? I was afraid we should never see you again."

"I feared so myself," said Tom, "but I have been saved in a wonderful manner. Has the train moved on?"

"Do you think we would go on without you? Not a man was willing to stir till you were found. Even Peabody, though afraid of falling into the hands of the Indians, and losing his scalp, was in favor of our waiting. The boys are very anxious about you."

Tom heard this with satisfaction. The esteem of our friends and associates is dear to us all, and it is always sad to think that we may be forgotten in absence.

"But you have not told me of your escape, Tom," said Miles. "Where are the Indians who captured you?"

"All dead!" answered Tom solemnly.

"Good heavens! You don't mean to say -- "

"That I killed them? Oh, no! Look over there! Can you see anything?"

Miles looked earnestly.

"I think I see upon the ground some men and horses."

"It is the Indians. They were pursuing me when they were trampled to death by a herd of buffaloes."

"Wonderful!" cried Miles. "I have heard of such things but hardly believed in them."

"It was a terrible sight," said Tom soberly. "I wish I could have been saved in some other way."

"It was you or they," said Miles sententiously. "It is well as it is."

They were warmly welcomed at the camp. Tom was looked upon as one raised from the dead, and the particulars of his wonderful escape were called for again and again.

"You are sure they didn't scalp you, Tom?" asked Mr. Peabody.

"Feel and see, Mr. Peabody," said Tom, smiling. "I believe my hair is pretty firm."

"I wouldn't have been in your shoes for all the gold in California," said Peabody fervently.

"I believe you, Mr. Peabody. Indeed, I think I may say that I wouldn't be placed in the same situation again for all the gold in the world."

"Tom," said Scott, "you are bound to succeed."

"What makes you think so?"

"You have shown so much pluck and coolness that you are sure to get along."

"I hope so, I am sure, for my father's sake."

Some weeks later a wagon-train was seen slowly climbing a mountain pass on the crest of the Sierra Nevada Mountains. They reached the summit, and, looking eagerly to the westward, saw the land of gold at their feet. They had spent months in reaching it. Now it lay spread before them, glorious in the sunlight.

"Yonder lies the promised land, my lad," said Ferguson. "It remains to be seen whether we shall be rewarded for our long and toilsome journey."

"If hard work will win success, I mean to succeed," said Tom stoutly.

"I don't see any gold," said Lawrence Peabody, with a disappointed air.

"Did you think it grew on trees, Mr. Peabody?" asked Scott sarcastically.

"I should like to stop a week at a first-class hotel before getting to work," remarked Peabody. "I don't like roughing it."

"We will leave you at the first hotel of that sort we meet. Now, boys, gather about me, and give three rousing cheers for California."

Thus spoke Miles and swung his hat. The cheers were given with a will, and the wagon-train commenced the descent.

THE END

~ ~ ~

TEACHERS GUIDE QUESTIONS FOR THE YOUNG ADVENTURER

1. Horatio Alger portrays or describes people in ways that were commonplace during his time, but that we would never use today.

   a. How has the meaning or "appropriateness" of the language that Alger used changed today? What does this teach you about the historical aspect of this time period?

   b. In what ways, as an individual and as a society, has our choice of words changed?

   c. In the same way in which Alger's words were considered common language but are now not, how do you think our language will change in the future? What words or phrases commonly used today do you think will one day be considered racist, taboo, crude or inappropriate?

2. In the opening chapters, how does Mrs. Nelson define happiness? How do you think Tom embodies this concept of happiness throughout the story?

3. In Chapter II, Tom finds a wallet on the road. What would you do if you had found the wallet? Why would you take this course of action?

4. Mr. Nelson agrees that Tom is at a pivotal age where he should start to explore life away from the farm.

   a. Do you agree or disagree that it is important for young men and young women to leave home in order to expand their experiences and opportunities? Why or why not?

   b. Instead of traveling out west in search of gold, how and at what age do youth sometimes take certain rights of passage away from home today?

5. Alger refers to Tom as "green." What does the author mean by this word? Support your answer by describing two instances when Tom displays his "greenness."

6. In Chapter VI, the reader is introduced to Milton Graham. What are the first clues that he is not the person he claims to be? How does he try to swindle Tom in the subsequent chapters?

7. The reader is first introduced to Mr. Nicholas Waterbury in Pittsburg. How do Tom and Mr. Waterbury become acquainted? How does their relationship develop, and in what ways does Mr. Waterbury help Tom?

8. Tom continues to offer his services during the team's trip out west. In what ways are Mr. Peabody's and Tom's characters and courage different? Give examples to contrast their personalities and abilities.

9. What is Tom's overall outlook on life? How does he confront trying situations during his entire journey out west?

10. Do you think Tom will succeed in his quest for gold and his desire to help his family? Why or why not?

TEACHERS GUIDE ANSWERS FOR THE YOUNG ADVENTURER

1. Some of the words that Alger uses are considered racist or inappropriate today. For example, he refers to Indians as "dirty savages."

 b. When Alger lumps entire groups of people together and makes observations about them, he uses language that reflects how many Americans thought. Alger assumes that all Bostonians, save for Peabody, are strong and hardworking. He writes that all Indians are savages and that Scotsmen, save for Ferguson, like to drink. Today it is generally expected that we steer away from negative and broad generalizations.

2. Mrs. Nelson states that, "Money is not happiness." Though Tom does want to earn gold to help his family, he looks for happiness in other things: through new friendships, through adventure and the unknown and through his desire to help others, including his family.

4. Youth today can take several rights of passage away from home: going away to college, traveling abroad with or without their family, celebrating bar/bat mitzvahs and more.

5. When Alger describes Tom as "green," he implies that he is less experienced and knowledgeable about city life and the outside world because he comes from the country. Tom displays his greenness first when he meets Milton Graham, believes he has good intentions and divulges information about his travels. Later, Graham uses this information to try and swindle Tom. Tom displays his greenness again when he reveals to the clerk at the Pittsburgh house where he keeps his money. Though the clerk does not have ill intentions, he advises Tom to be more prudent and not so trusting of strangers.

6. The first clue that Graham is not who he claims to be is when Tom finds out that Graham lied about the cheaper cost of board by sharing a room. The second clue is when Tom speaks with the clerk at the Pittsburgh house and the clerk advises him to be careful and guard his money. Graham tries to swindle Tom first by searching his belongings for Tom's money and secondly by trying to plant counterfeit money on Tom and blame Tom for Graham's theft.

7.   Tom is walking around Pittsburgh when he bumps into Mr. Waterbury, who is intoxicated. Tom helps the drunken man return safely to the hotel and to his room. The next day, Mr. Waterbury is eternally grateful, and he realizes that Tom is a genuine, honest and trustworthy boy. Mr. Waterbury acts as Tom's guardian for the remainder of their travels together. Mr. Waterbury helps Tom when he confronts Graham regarding the theft of the counterfeit money and warns him to leave Tom alone.

8.   Mr. Peabody's and Tom's characters and courage differ in several ways. Mr. Peabody is constantly complaining about the voyage, his constitution and the prospects ahead. He is so terrified of Indians that he tries numerous ways to escape night watch of camp. His expectations for gold were grand, but he is not realistic or willing to work hard to earn the gold. Tom, on the other hand, is enthusiastic for the journey and the prospects that lie ahead. He is more than willing to help at every opportunity, and he treats the difficulties as forms of new adventure. He is optimistic, hard-working and brave when confronted by Indians and other dangers.

9.   Tom's overall outlook on life is to stay positive, work hard and treat every new situation like an adventure. He confronts trying situations, such as being captured by Indians, with intelligent action and grit.

COMMENTARY FOR
THE YOUNG ADVENTURER AND
THE YOUNG MINER

by Rick Newcombe

While the early Horatio Alger stories took place in New York City, some of the later stories were set on the West Coast or they focused on traveling from New York to San Francisco in the 1870s. The Young Adventurer is mainly about the journey, while The Young Miner shows us what happens after they arrive.

Thomas Nelson is the hero of both books. We follow his exploits as he travels more than 3,000 miles by train, steamboat and horseback, all when he is barely 16 years old. This was an era before planes and automobiles had even been invented.

Tom's "Stories of Success" are absolutely amazing, and they are pure Horatio Alger.

We first meet Tom when he is with his father, mother, brothers and sisters on their dirt-poor farm in New Hampshire. We learn that the richest man in town, Squire Hudson, is cruel and heartless, while Tom's struggling father, Mark Nelson, is warm and loving. These are not unusual characterizations -- of nasty rich people and kind poor people -- in Horatio Alger stories.

Despite the widespread misconception that Horatio Alger was an advocate for the rich, Alger's view of money was far more nuanced. Wealth can be great, he said, and it can be awful. It can be used for good: to feed the hungry, for instance; and it can be used for evil: to force a family out of their home.

Mark Nelson's heart is filled with love and happiness, particularly since his wife, who was known as Mary Dale when they met, is so beautiful and cheerful. We learn that Squire Hudson still harbors a grudge because he wanted to marry her, but she said no and chose Mark Nelson instead. Hudson secretly vows to get even by plotting to drive the Nelsons off their farm and into the poorhouse. "When she and her children are paupers, she may regret the slight she put upon me," he says to himself.

Alger's writing style is witty, his plots are ingenious and his dialogue is clear, easy to understand and, at times, brilliant. For instance, when he wants to tell the reader that Squire Hudson's wife is not beautiful compared with Mary Nelson, he does so by allowing us to hear the squire's thoughts. His wife is talking about Mrs. Nelson, and says she is with Mark Nelson only because she did not have any other proposals of marriage, not knowing that her own husband had proposed to Mary.

The squire replied:

"'Probably she did (have other proposals), for she was a very pretty girl.'

"'Then she's faded,' said Mrs. Hudson, tossing her head.

"Squire Hudson did not reply; but as his eyes rested on the sharp, querulous face of his helpmate, and he compared it mentally with the pleasant face of Mrs. Nelson, he said to himself that, faded or not, the latter was still better looking than his wife had been in the days of her youth. Of course it would not do to say so, for Mrs. Hudson was not amiable."

Tom senses danger for his family during their discussion about finances, and he wants to do something about it. His sister and father comment about the unequal distribution of wealth. It doesn't seem fair that one family would have so much and another so little. But Horatio Alger was no socialist, and Americans in the 1870s looked to their own initiative -- not government handouts -- for creating wealth.

Publisher's Weekly magazine asserts that Horatio Alger helped form the American character, and in the 21st century, we still strive for material success through hard work, rather than taking it from others. As the columnist Charles Krauthammer said, "Americans, generally speaking, don't envy the rich. They want to be rich."

There was little chance for Tom to get rich or help his family financially if he stayed on the New Hampshire farm. It appears that the family had already moved once, from New Jersey. But this time Tom knew he would have to travel west to find his fortune. The California gold rush was in the newspapers, and Tom set a goal to join the thousands of other prospectors.

He had no money to buy tickets for traveling such a long distance. How could he possibly even begin? Horatio Alger tells us: "The world was all before him where to choose. His available capital was small, it is true, amounting only to thirty-seven cents and a jack-knife; but he had, besides, a stout heart, a pair of strong hands, an honest face, and plenty of perseverance -- not bad equipment for a young adventurer."

This was Horatio Alger's way of telling us that the intangible virtues of courage, strength, honesty and perseverance are more important than money. If you live your life with these virtues, the money will follow.

The issue of honesty comes up repeatedly in both books, which is not surprising, considering that most Americans view honesty as one of the most important character traits of successful people. For instance, we have all heard the stories about George Washington admitting to chopping down a cherry tree, saying, "I cannot tell a lie," and Abraham Lincoln walking a long distance to return some change after a store clerk had given him too much. True or not, they are part of this nation's mythology.

Tom Nelson's honesty does not always pay off immediately -- in fact, at one point it looks like he might be put in jail -- but in the end, honesty does prove to be the best policy.

Tom has remarkable courage. He takes calculated risks in a series of thrilling adventures in both books, and he succeeds over and over.

Throughout the stories, Horatio Alger creates characters with opposing character traits, which helps the reader see the contrast between right and wrong. For instance, we see Sinclair Hudson, the arrogant son of the squire, who is lazy and envious while Tom is industrious and generous. We see the swindlers and thieves, Milton Graham and his friend Vincent, and Bill Crane in another episode, all of whom keep tripping over themselves and failing in their devious designs.

We see other thieves in The Young Miner, including two Chinese men, who are referred to as "heathens" and "Chinamen," which was typical of the times. Mark Twain wrote a newspaper story defending Chinese workers in Northern California, and he referred to them as "Chinamen," which I'm sure he meant as a term of endearment. Today, that word is considered offensive, but in the 1870s, it was not.

Native Americans don't fare much better. Native Americans were called "savages" and worse in the writings of the time, so it is not surprising to see similar descriptions in Horatio Alger stories.

The last Horatio Alger novel was written years before the passage of Prohibition, and we have no idea what Alger's political views on the subject were, but it is clear that the author was anti-alcohol in his own life. He creates a realistic fight scene in a saloon involving a temperance man from Scotland, Donald Ferguson, and a fall-down drunk American who is totally obnoxious in the Missouri tavern. Alger also was resolutely opposed to tobacco, though an occasional praiseworthy character can be seen enjoying a pipe after dinner. It was mainly the boys and young men who spent their money on cigars while visiting pool halls and saloons that he mocked.

Wearing nice clothes was so important during this time period. If you were poor, you wore rags. If you had some money, you could afford nice clothes. As part of that emphasis on appearance, a pocket watch, or vest watch, was considered a status symbol. When Tom acquires one as a gift, he agrees with his donor, Mr. Waterbury, that on the first day he will check the time every few minutes, just as Mr. Waterbury did when he was a young man with his first watch.

Let me offer two unrelated comments about the vest watch because I believe it carries great significance. First, it is important that Tom had asked his mother to sew in an extra pocket for this watch, although at the time he had neither a watch nor even the slightest prospect of obtaining one. Still, he had faith and optimism. He expected that someday he would indeed have such a watch. By having his mother sew the pocket in his vest, he was using what we today call "visualization" to achieve his goal.

Paul J. Meyer, founder of the company Success Motivation Institute, recorded a powerful speech called "The Power of Goal Setting," in which he talked about the importance of expecting positive results. He cited Charles Kettering's "birdcage theory." Kettering headed up the research department at General Motors for 20 years and was responsible for the electrical starting motor and leaded gasoline. He said that if you were to buy a birdcage and put it in your room, it would be only a matter of time before you succumbed and put a bird in it. Along the same lines, Tom Nelson had asked his mother to sew in a pocket for his vest watch, which created a constant reminder, a forced visualization, of what he wanted, and it was only a matter of time before he got the watch.

Horatio Alger was a century and a half ahead of today's motivational writers, who say the same thing but probably are unaware that they are standing on his shoulders. If you want a contemporary example, look at this passage from Rhonda Byrne's bestselling book, The Secret, which was first published in 2006. She tells the story of a woman who found her "perfect partner" by doing precisely what Tom Nelson's mother did for him by sewing that pocket:

"Then one day as she arrived home and was parking her car in the middle of her garage, she gasped as she realized that her actions were contradicting what she wanted. If her car was in the middle of the garage, there was no room for her perfect partner's car! Her actions were powerfully saying to the Universe that she did not believe she was going to receive what she had asked for. So she immediately cleaned up her garage and parked her car to one side, leaving space for her perfect partner's car on the other side."

The second observation involves the issue of how so many things of the past come back in a different form in the present. Isn't it interesting how, for more than a century after the Horatio Alger stories were first printed, most people checked the time by wearing wristwatches? They would not reach into their pockets to find a timepiece. Yet, in the 21st century, if you ask someone the time, more often than not they will reach into their pockets to check the time on their smart phone.

This is one of the most fascinating aspects of reading Horatio Alger stories -- to see America as it was between 1865 and 1900. This was a time when nearly everyone was consumed with getting rich. Mark Twain called it the "Gilded Age." Reading the Horatio Alger Series gives many details of America at the time, both externally -- the hardships, the crudeness of life without running water or electricity -- and internally, which includes the way they thought. This has been called the "climate of opinion." Money was a constant topic of conversation, and government was hardly mentioned at all. For many years after the Civil War, the federal government in Washington, D.C., was not an important part of the lives of most Americans.

At the end of The Young Miner, we see that Tom is indeed on the path to great riches. He has been able to help his family out, and he is totally independent, becoming a wealthy merchant in San Francisco. (If you want to know the value of his wealth in today's dollars, Google the words "inflation calculator," and you will find a number of websites that will help you calculate the answer.)

He also shows a generous spirit by giving the hapless Sinclair Hudson money as a favor because he is so downtrodden.

Tom Nelson lives his life with an air of "positive expectancy." He is always cheerful and optimistic. He is poised and confident. For instance, when a servant tells him to go to the back door, he politely stands his ground. He embraces hard work. He is courageous when encountering new adventures, even when it looks like the American Indians might kill him.

In other words, he is the original embodiment of the values embraced in what has become, over the years, a multibillion-dollar self-improvement industry. Horatio Alger spelled out the keys to success and happiness, not with a list of rules or principles, but by creating the ideal boy as he becomes a man. He called his central characters "heroes" because they represent the ultimate personification of the ideal young man, as he grows from adolescence, on his exciting and prosperous adventures in these inspiring "Stories of Success."

Rick Newcombe is the founder and CEO of Creators Syndicate, Creators Publishing and Sumner Books.

THE LIFE AND THEMES OF

HORATIO ALGER, JR.

By Stefan Kanfer

The Merriam-Webster Dictionary devotes one sentence to him: "Of, relating to, or resembling the fiction of Horatio Alger in which success is achieved through self-reliance and hard work."

True as far as it goes, but that sentence reveals nothing about the man or his accomplishment. Then again, other contemporary reference books are just as terse. Not one acknowledges that Alger in his day (circa 1880-1920) was a publishing phenomenon. During those decades, when a sale of 10,000 volumes was deemed a triumph, readers bought more than 200 million copies of Alger's works, placing him in a league with J.K. Rowling and Stephen King.

Alas, today most of his novels—and there are more than 100—are out of print. But not for long. Thanks to the resuscitation efforts of Sumner Books, a division of Creators Syndicate, Alger's best literary productions are being furnished with fresh covers, new fonts and energetic promotion.

Seldom has there been a more relevant illustration of the maxim that what goes around comes around. At the turn of the 19th century, Alger was the standard-bearer of a phenomenally successful experiment in social reform and personal improvement. That movement inspired disadvantaged kids to move on up, leading juvenile delinquents into productive, significant lives. Men as different as Groucho Marx and Ernest Hemingway were fans.

"Horatio Alger's books conveyed a powerful message to me," wrote Marx, "and to many of my young friends as well—that if you worked hard at your trade, the big chance would eventually come. As a child I didn't regard it as a myth, and as an old man I think of it as the story of my life."

Hemingway's sister Marcelline recalled that during their childhood, "There was one summer when Ernest couldn't get enough of Horatio Alger." Not that Alger's boys' books influenced Papa's prose style. But there must have been something in the writer's stress on grit and self-reliance that affected young Ernest, as it did so many of his contemporaries.

By the end of the Roaring Twenties, though, Horatio Alger had become as passé as the Ford Model T. During the Depression he fared no better; Nathaniel West's satirical 1934 novel, A Cool Million, sent Alger's plots in reverse, as the naïve protagonist loses limb after limb seeking success among rapacious capitalists. Decades later, the film adaptation of Hunter Thompson's 1971 novel, Fear and Loathing in Las Vegas, presented the antihero as "Horatio Alger gone mad on drugs in Las Vegas."

What lay behind Alger's ability to enchant so many Americans—and to enrage so many others? The author's story furnishes a trove of clues:

The sickly child of a Unitarian minister in Marlborough, Massachusetts, Horatio, born in 1832, was always the smallest in his class and far from an academic star. Still, his report cards were good enough for admission to Harvard. There his academic prowess was in inverse proportion to his size (5 feet 2 inches). He won prizes, published verse and fiction in undergraduate magazines, and labeled the entire four years a period of "unmixed happiness."

Decades would pass before he found such contentment again. Upon graduation, Horatio attempted to make his way as a writer. After five unsuccessful years, he returned to Harvard, this time to study at the Divinity School. In 1860 the Reverend Horatio Alger was named minister of the First Parish Unitarian Church of Brewster on Cape Cod. Salary: $800 per year. To supplement his meager income, he turned once again to writing. This time, his stories were well-received, and he allowed himself to dream of a dual career of preacher and writer. That's when catastrophe struck.

It was of his own making, if one historian is to be believed. According to this claim, a 13-year-old told his parents that the new parson had made advances to him. An investigation began. Another lad made a similar complaint. Faced with charges of behaving inappropriately, the accused was allowed to resign—with the proviso that he leave town at once.

Sometime later, Horatio wrote a poem about one Friar Anselmo, who had committed an unspecified crime. Melancholy and remorseful, he comes across a wounded traveler and gives him aid. Whereupon an angel materializes and offers salvation:

Thy guilty stains shall be washed white again
By noble service done thy fellow man.

The fugitive repaired to New York City in the spring of 1866, resolved to live out the Christian ideal, expiating his sin by saving others. The Manhattan he entered was the epicenter of the Gilded Age, a magnet for millions of ambitious climbers, drawn by the post-Civil War boom. Out of sight of the glittering prosperity, the mansions and carriages, however, was another New York, a squalid night town that travelers compared to Calcutta, India.

In The Good Old Days, They Were Terrible, historian Otto Bettmann reports that there was scarcely a slum that pedestrians could negotiate "without climbing over a heap of trash or, in rain, wading through a bed of slime." Many streets were so dangerous that policemen hesitated to walk them alone. A Gramercy Park resident noted in his diary, "Most of my friends are investing in revolvers and carry them about at night"—and the Park was one of the city's better neighborhoods.

The New York City street urchin entered the national consciousness in those years. More than 60,000 neglected or abandoned kids ran unsupervised in the street, partly because of the fallout from the tidal waves of immigration from Europe and partly because of families broken by the Civil War.

What was to be done about these juveniles likely to die on the streets or to end up behind bars? The Reverend Charles Loring Brace founded the Children's Aid Society, designed to take homeless or abused kids away from their corrosive environments. At the same time, John Hughes, New York's first Roman Catholic archbishop, set up parochial schools and a residential institution called the Catholic Protectory, which brought up abandoned or orphaned children to be useful members of society.

Horatio Alger joined these efforts at reclamation. He, too, asked himself what could be done about homeless children. Seeking answers, he wandered through the city's worst neighborhoods. He interviewed "street arabs" who spoke of broken homes, violent confrontations with parents, doomed futures. He observed how their cocky attitudes masked a profound despair. He advised them to get real jobs instead of hanging about, squandering whatever came their way from shining shoes or picking pockets. A handful nodded in agreement, expressing the desire to change their lives; most were content to take life as they found it.

Why, he pondered, did individuals subjected to the same conditions turn out so differently? One boy might become a thief, a sociopath, even a killer. His neighbor, perhaps his brother, might aim to be an upright citizen. What was the difference between them?

What saved certain boys, he came to believe, was a quality that gave them the strength to resist sloth and temptation. In a word, character. But was this inborn? In that case determinism won the day, and change was out of the question. Or, given the right opportunity and attitude, could a dispossessed youth win his share of the American dream? The latter, Alger believed—but only if the boy stopped regarding himself as a victim.

As Alger meditated upon the worst crime of the slums—the stealing of childhood from children—an idea came to him. He would be Brother Anselmo redivivus. He had sinned against youths; now he would rescue them—and in the process save himself. As the novelist put it, by depicting the situation of city waifs, he would "excite a deeper and more widespread sympathy in the public mind, as well as exert a salutary influence upon the class of whom he is writing, by setting before them inspiring examples of what energy, ambition, and an honest purpose may achieve."

Ragged Dick became the template of the fiction to follow. Subtitled Street Life in New York with the Boot Blacks, it charted the rise of a 14-year-old boy from poverty to prosperity. Dick Hunter is an adolescent with all odds against him. He has no family, he smokes, drinks alcohol when he can afford it—not very often on the small change he gets from shining gentlemen's shoes—and sleeps on gratings in the winter.

Yet something separates him from his fellow waifs. He refuses to pick pockets like the others, won't mock his elders, and yearns to "grow up 'spectable.'" His bearing and his innate decency attract the attention of upright New Yorkers. One introduces him to his church; another presents Dick with a few dollars.

The earnest youth resolves to become literate to save his money and live a clean life. One day on a walk near South Ferry he sees a toddler fall in the water. Without hesitation, Dick jumps in and saves the drowning child. In gratitude, the father, an affluent businessman, offers the rescuer a job in his office. Gainfully employed, the onetime vagabond Dick Hunter becomes Richard Hunter Esq., and shuts the door forever on the "old vagabond life which he hoped never to resume."

Naïve? Simplistic? To the jaded, the cynical and the ignorant, yes. But not to thousands of children trapped in the real world of poverty and early death. They got the message of Ragged Dick and demanded more Horatio Alger novels with more moral lessons for them to absorb. Those books changed—and in many cases saved— lives a century before Dr. Martin Luther King Jr. stated his belief that what mattered was not the color of one's skin but the content of one's character.

Today, if you listen closely you can hear, amid the jeers, the escalating sound of the last laugh. In 1947, the Horatio Alger Association was founded. It attracts more prominent men and women now than it did then. The group is dedicated to recognizing American leaders who rose, like Alger's young heroes, from humble origins "through honesty, hard work, self-reliance and perseverance." With grants to U.S. high-school students who have "faced and overcome great obstacles in their young lives," the association encourages them to emulate such enterprising and disparate members as Oprah Winfrey and Ray Kroc, Tom Brokaw and Maya Angelou, Stan Musial and Colin Powell.

They can all testify to the truths that lie between the covers of this volume. Turn the first few pages, and you'll understand why so many followed Horatio Alger's breathless, cliff-hanging chapters leading the way from skid row to success. And why so many more are about to read that map in a world where everything has changed—except the basic truths of life.

Stefan Kanfer is an award-winning writer for City Journal and the author of numerous best-selling books.

ABOUT HORATIO ALGER, JR.

Horatio Alger was born in 1832 in Chelsea, Massachusetts. He spent his early years in the small town and under the guidance of the church and his father, the town pastor, before the family moved just west of Boston to the town of Marlborough.

As a shy young boy, Alger poured himself into books and soon became a distinguished student. He studied at Harvard and Harvard Divinity School before becoming a minister. He practiced ministry for a few years near Boston and on Cape Cod, but he was distracted by his true passion: writing.

He loved to write, and by 1865 Alger had written a handful of stories, including Frank's Campaign and Paul Prescott's Charge. The latter was the first in a series of stories that would eventually lead to his great success. In 1866, Alger moved to New York to write poetry, newspaper stories and magazine articles. However, he was shocked to find so many homeless and forgotten children among the streets, an unfortunate consequence of the Civil War. He made it his duty to aid the condition of these lost children, both through his stories and by his continuous acts of benevolence.

Horatio Alger became a household name shortly after the Civil War when he began publishing stories in the form of serializations. These serializations were featured in magazines such as Student and Schoolmate and were later compiled as books. Alger's books became enormously popular, especially among teenage boys across the country, and they soon reached millions and millions of readers. Alger continued to produce several stories a year, and, in later years, wrote novels in and of themselves instead of novels from magazine serials.

The years immediately following the Civil War were the same years when the United States emerged as one nation on the road to becoming a worldwide empire. The years between 1865 and 1900 were the years of the empire builders, with the rags-to-riches stories of John D. Rockefeller, Andrew Carnegie, Cornelius Vanderbilt and Thomas Edison. They were the years that laid the foundation for Henry Ford and other business titans and for the spectacular growth of the American economy throughout the 20th century and through today. During these years, Alger published well over 100 stories, poems and novels that spoke to the timeless themes and successes of this era.

The theme of Alger's books is consistent: If you work hard, go the extra mile, are faithful and honest, show kindness and generosity, and maintain a cheerful, positive and optimistic attitude, you will succeed in creating financial security and happiness. On the other hand, if you lie, cheat, steal, are lazy or envious, and try to take advantage of other people, you will be doomed to failure and misery. Despite his background as a preacher, Alger does not make these points in a self-righteous or pontificating way. What he does instead -- just like the parables that Jesus told -- is to create stories that illustrate the virtues that lead to success. And the stories that Alger creates are no ordinary stories. Each one is filled with lively plots and twists and turns, ones that are always unexpected and keep the reader wanting to know what's going to happen next.

As Alger grew older, he continuously strived to write the Great American Novel, little realizing that the rags-to-riches stories he created were more influential than any other novelists'. He travelled out west in early 1877 searching for new material and returned near the end of the year, producing similar stories with a new western backdrop. By 1897, Alger was suffering from asthma, bronchitis and slight short-term memory loss. He moved in with his sister in South Natick, Massachusetts where he spent the last two years of his life.

Most people have never heard of Horatio Alger while some are vaguely familiar with the term "rags-to-riches." In the Alger family, it was the norm to burn correspondence and manuscripts, and this, coupled with Alger's shyness, has greatly kept him from history's limelight. Though too often forgotten today, Alger's works and the themes within them still affect the American psyche. Many assert that there is a lagging spirit in present American culture, that these inspiring stories are irrelevant. Young people are bombarded with external stimuli that make it difficult for them to get to know themselves. Wide-eyed innocence and childlike enthusiasm, once revered as admirable qualities, are sources of mockery and disdain, which makes cynicism and pessimism inevitable. Video games, television shows, movies and music are all aimed at titillating and at seeing who can be the most gritty, violent or shocking. More than a few commentators have used the word "degrading" to describe the assault that children encounter today.

This is unfortunate. Young people need heroes and role models today just as much as they did in the 1870s and '80s, when Alger was creating them at a feverish pace from his New York City apartment, writing as many as four books at a time. Publisher A.K. Loring asserted that Alger's books "captured the spirits of reborn America" for "above all you can hear the cry of triumph of the oppressed over the oppressor … What Alger has done is to portray the soul – the ambitious soul – of the country." Years later, biographer Edwin P. Hoyt concludes that Alger is "a writer whose influence on the American scene has been so profound that it is hard to measure." Indeed, Alger's works made an overwhelming impression on American culture and society that are still alive with us today. It is for this reason that these classics must be brought to a new generation of readers.

OUR COMMITMENT TO
HORATIO ALGER

By Rick Newcombe

Sumner Books is totally committed to reviving interest in Horatio Alger, one of the best-selling authors of all time yet someone who has been all but forgotten today. I'd like to tell you how this project came about.

Probably the best starting point is to tell you a little about myself. I grew up in suburban Chicago, and my parents were religious and fundamentally optimistic in their outlook on life. They encouraged all eight of their children to be positive in our thinking and hope and pray for the best in all situations. In my adolescence, I discovered many of the self-help authors from the 20th century, including Dale Carnegie, Napoleon Hill and Norman Vincent Peale. I remember reading a small magazine in the 1970s, when I was in my 20s, called Success Unlimited and being inspired each month to work hard and stay positive. The publisher of this magazine was W. Clement Stone, who started his career selling insurance policies door to door and who went on to build Combined Insurance, which became part of Aon, one of the largest insurance companies in the world.

By the time Mr. Stone died in 2002, he was a very successful businessman, an extremely generous philanthropist and totally committed to spreading the gospel of positive thinking. I remember reading one of his books, The Success System That Never Fails, which was both an autobiography and a blueprint for achieving success. Stone told the story of spending a summer on a farm in Michigan when he was 12, getting fresh air, helping on the farm and enjoying picnics, carnivals and camping out.

W. Clement Stone

"But I'll never forget the first day I went upstairs to the attic," he wrote, "for there I met Horatio Alger. At least 50 of his books, dusty and weather-worn, were piled in the corner. I took one down to the hammock in the front yard and started to read."

Stone said he was so enthralled he couldn't stop. "I read through all of them that summer," he wrote.

He said the principle in each book was that "the hero became a success because he was a man of character -- the villain a failure because he deceived and embezzled. How many Alger books were sold? No one knows. Estimates range from 100 million to 300 million. We do know that his books inspired thousands of American boys from poor families to strive to do the right thing because it was right and to acquire wealth."

That was the first time I had heard of Horatio Alger, but it never occurred to me to try to find his books. Over the years, I founded Creators Syndicate, which became one of the most successful newspaper syndication companies in the world. I attribute much of our success to our positive thinking and upbeat attitude. We became a multimillion-dollar international corporation by syndicating a wide variety of journalists, celebrities and award-winning cartoonists.

As we were expanding into new businesses, e-books and audiobooks were a natural starting point because we work with so many talented writers and artists. But we also wanted to try new things. With that in mind, I remembered Mr. Stone's enthusiastic recommendation of Horatio Alger's books, and I decided to read some. Many were available as e-books, and I thoroughly enjoyed them.an

I had a good feeling whenever I was transported back to New York City as it was in 1870, when trains were called "cars" and there were no automobiles. There was a constant risk of crossing the streets without streetlights or walk signs. A number of years later, the Brooklyn Dodgers, now the Los Angeles Dodgers, got their name from the treacherous dodging of horses, wagons and streetcars that was required to cross the street in the city. In those days, plumbing with hot and cold running water was not taken for granted, much less radios, televisions, computers or smartphones. Are you kidding? A smartphone in the 1860s? There wasn't even a telephone.

But what great stories Alger wrote -- one after another. I couldn't get enough of them! And it was impossible not to feel grateful for all the modern conveniences of the 21st century when immersing myself in the world of America as it was in the 1860s and '70s.

As I read book after book, I felt like a teenager all over again, excited about the future and the promise of a brighter tomorrow. It was then that I decided to go full bore into spreading the word of Horatio Alger.

One of the problems with the e-books was the lack of organization; another was the maddening number of typos, over and over and over, or the lack of illustrations or the lack of a table of contents. In fact, what was intended to be a good deed to spread Mr. Alger's message really turned out to be something of a disservice.

So I made it my mission to have professional editors edit the texts so there were no typographical or spelling errors. We found appropriate illustrations. We included detailed tables of contents for each book, and we decided to publish them in groups, when appropriate, which has never been done before. We are including commentaries and teachers guides with each e-book.

We also decided to make audiobooks of as many of these "Stories of Success" as possible. We hired a terrific actor, Ben Gillman, and his initial experience shows you how far we have to go to spread the word. Ben went to the Hollywood public library to find some Horatio Alger books, but there was none. "You'd have to go to the downtown public library, in the historical section, to find those," the librarian told him.

Remember, this is one of the best-selling American authors of all time, yet it is as if he never existed.

Part of the problem is that some of the caricatures of Horatio Alger over the years have been absolutely brutal. Even to this day, the Encyclopedia Britannica, from which we expect objective reporting, calls Alger's dialogue and plots "outrageously bad." Come again? The encyclopedia is supposed to provide broad knowledge on specific subjects, not offer the biased literary criticism of a handful of editors. Talk about being unfair -- and just plain wrong!

How do you answer a cheap shot like that? Really, it is nothing more than an incredibly snooty opinion; in fact, it is an "outrageously bad" opinion. Remember, the Horatio Alger books were intended to be not great literature but rather inspirational stories to motivate young boys to achieve a better life. If the dialogue and plots were not lively and believable, the books would not have sold in the millions. The fact that Horatio Alger helped form the American character shows that an incredible number of boys ate up his books as thrilling and believable.

The brilliant writer Stefan Kanfer wrote an extensive review of Horatio Alger's works in 2000 for City Journal magazine, a publication of the prestigious Manhattan Institute. He started off believing the critics, but when he actually read some of Horatio Alger's books, he drew a totally different conclusion. "I began reading the novels aloud to my children," he wrote. "We found them well-plotted, entertaining, and instructive, not at all the righteous antiquities that I had been led to believe. Almost every chapter ends with a cliff-hanger, and all of us could hardly wait for the next night to find out what happened. The conclusions never failed to produce an emotional satisfaction and a feeling that what the author was selling -- independence, forbearance, square dealing -- was well worth buying."

We can only speculate about why the critics have been so harsh on Horatio Alger, but no doubt some it stems from their being turned off by precisely the character traits that Mr. Kanfer identifies. Like it or not, there is a mindset that scoffs at individual achievement through hard work, a positive attitude and generosity -- living every day with an "attitude of gratitude," which is the essence of Horatio Alger's message.

W. Clement Stone was routinely mocked for starting the day by saying, "I feel healthy! I feel happy! I feel terrific!" He encouraged his employees to do the same. In fact, he encouraged everyone to demonstrate outward enthusiasm and PMA, which stood for a positive mental attitude. His critics thought he was ridiculous, but Mr. Stone got the last laugh, living to age 100, which he had set as his goal, and accumulating hundreds of millions of dollars.

Roswell Crawford is an important character in Ragged Dick and Fame and Fortune because he oozes the world-owes-me-a-living attitude that is so common today. "Roswell was troubled with a large share of pride," Alger writes, "though it might have troubled himself to explain what he had to be proud of."

Roswell never understands the importance of integrity and its relationship to earning one's living. In fact, he once says that he would be happy to be paid $10 a week for nothing. "Well, if I get it, I don't care if I don't earn it," he says. In fact, Roswell is ashamed to be seen in the streets carrying a large bundle as part of a delivery for his job. Before being fired, his boss tells him, "You appear to think yourself of too great consequence to discharge properly the duties of your position."

Contrast that with Richard Hunter's attitude toward his entry-level job when he first starts working at the firm. "I'm ready to do anything that is required of me. I want to make myself useful," he says.

I have the impression that was the same attitude that Horatio Alger had as he approached his goal of becoming a successful writer who could change the world -- or at least the world of the thousands of homeless street urchins in the big city. It is difficult to imagine how bad their plight was. For instance, in 1874, which was seven years after Ragged Dick was first published, there was a little girl named Mary Ellen Wilson, who was beaten unmercifully by her stepmother. She was sent out into the streets ill-clothed in winter. There were other abuses, and they were horrible.

So a social worker named Etta Angel Wheeler wanted to intervene, to help get the child out of that environment. But there were no laws to protect children in such situations. Etta was desperate -- and clever. She enlisted the help of the American Society for the Prevention of Cruelty to Animals because animals were protected by law. Her attorneys argued that Mary Ellen, "as a member of the animal kingdom, deserved the same protection as abused animals." This led to new legislation and various child protective services.

Horatio Alger was at the forefront of this movement. He wanted to help the poor kids in the inner city, and he wound up not only helping them but inspiring millions of other young readers across the country. Many of them transformed their lives as a direct result of the inspiration of the "Stories of Success" that Horatio Alger managed to tell in one exciting setting after another.

It is not surprising that Ernest Hemingway's sister said that her brother could not get enough of Horatio Alger or that Walter Brennan, a famous actor for much of the 20th century, devoured his books. As the legendary Groucho Marx said: "Horatio Alger's books conveyed a powerful message to me and to many of my young friends -- that if you worked hard at your trade, the big chance would eventually come. As a child, I didn't regard it as a myth, and as an old man, I think of it as the story of my life."

Groucho was speaking for millions of Americans in the past and, we hope, millions more in the future.

Rick Newcombe is the founder and CEO of Creators Syndicate, Creators Publishing and Sumner Books.

PREVIEW OF ANOTHER ADVENTURE IN THE HORATIO ALGER "STORIES OF SUCCESS" SERIES

THE YOUNG MINER

By Horatio Alger, Jr.

A dozen men, provided with gold rocker boxes, were busily engaged in gathering and washing dirt, mingled with gold dust, on the banks of a small stream in California. It was in the early days, and this party was but one of hundreds who were scattered over the new Eldorado, seeking the shining metal which throughout the civilized world exercises a potent and irresistible sway.

I have said there were a dozen men, but this is a mistake. One of the party was a well-grown boy of sixteen with a good-humored and even handsome face. He was something more than good-humored, however. There was an expression on his face which spoke of strength and resolution and patient endurance. The readers of "The Young Adventurer" will at once recognize in our young hero Tom Nelson, the oldest son of a poor New England farmer, who, finding no prospects at home, had joined the tide of immigrants pouring from all parts of the country to the land of which so many marvelous stories were told. Tom had come to work, and, though he doubtless shared to some extent the extravagant anticipations of the great body of Eastern visitors who hoped to make a fortune in a year, he did not expect to succeed without hard toil.

His companions belonged to the same party with whom he had crossed the plains, under the leadership of Phineas Fletcher, a broad-shouldered Illinois farmer, who had his family with him. Next to Tom was Donald Ferguson, a grave Scotchman and Tom's special friend -- a man of excellent principles, thoroughly reliable, and held in high respect by all, though not possessed of popular manners. On the other side was Lawrence Peabody, a young Boston clerk, who had spent several years behind a dry goods counter. He was soft and effeminate, with no talent for "roughing it" and wholly unfitted for the hard work that he had undertaken. He was deeply disappointed in his first work at gold-hunting, having come out with the vague idea that he should pick up a big nugget within a short time that would make his fortune and enable him to go home a rich man. The practical side of gold-seeking--this washing particles of dust from the dirt of the riverbed--was in the highest degree unsatisfactory and discouraging. He was not a bad fellow, and his companions, though they laughed at him, were well disposed towards him.

Among the rest, mention may be made of John Miles, Henry Scott, and Chapman, owner of a refractory donkey named after King Solomon.

Not far away from the river were the tents occupied by the miners. There was but one house, roughly built of logs. This was occupied by Captain Fletcher and his family. He had not had the trouble of building it for he had found it ready for occupation; a previous party, who had wandered farther down the river in search of richer washings, had constructed it. In fact, it was this building in which our party had decided to remain.

"There isn't much difference in places," said Fletcher. "We may as well stay here."

"Then why was it deserted?" suggested John Miles dubiously. "That's rather strange, isn't it, captain?"

"Not necessarily, Miles. You've been on berrying parties, haven't you, when at home?"

"Many a time."

"You've noticed that many of the pickers leave good places, just from love of novelty, and wander about the field, often faring worse than if they remained where they were?"

"That's so, captain."

"Then let us give this place a try. We'll make more working steady in a medium place than wandering here, there and everywhere."

So the whole party agreed to "give the place a try."

There had been no brilliant success as yet but fair luck. In six days Tom had washed out twenty-five dollars' worth of gold dust, in spite of his awkwardness and inexperience. Others had done better, but poor Lawrence Peabody had barely five dollars' worth to show.

It must be said, however, that he had not averaged more than two or three hours of real labor in every twenty-four. He spent the rest of the time wandering about aimlessly or sitting down and watching the labors of his companions, while he enlivened them by pathetic lamentations over his unfortunate position, so far away from Boston and the refining influences of civilization.

A little transcript of a conversation between Tom and himself will throw light upon the characters of both.

"This is beastly work," sighed Peabody, resting from his feet by no means arduous labors and looking over to Tom. "I tell you, it isn't fit for a gentleman."

"It is rather hard to keep one's hands clean, Mr. Peabody," said Tom, "but you mustn't think of the present. Think of the time when you will go home, your pockets full of gold."

"I don't see any prospect of it, Tom," sighed Peabody. "Here I've been hard at work for a week, and I haven't got over five dollars' worth of dust."

"I have five times as much," said Tom.

"Some people are lucky," said Peabody.

"You haven't worked like Tom," said the Scotchman plainly. "You haven't averaged over two hours a day, while Tom has worked eight or ten."

"I have worked till my back was likely to break," said the young man from Boston. "I am not accustomed to manual labor, Mr. Ferguson. My friend Tom has worked on a farm, while I have been engaged in mercantile pursuits. Oh, why did I leave Boston?!"

"I am sure I can't guess," said Ferguson dryly.

"I never expected anything like this."

"What did you expect, if I may be so bold as to inquire?"

"I thought I should find the gold in big nuggets worth thousands of dollars apiece. I was always reading in the papers about finding them. I think it's a great shame to deceive people by such stories. I don't believe there are any nuggets."

"Oh, yes, there are, but they are few and far between," said Fletcher. "A neighbor of mine found one worth three thousand dollars. Altogether he brought home five thousand dollars and invested it in a farm and sawmill. He has a good business. When he came to California he had nothing."

"That is what I should like, Captain Fletcher," said Tom. "If I could only manage to carry home five thousand dollars, I could make my father comfortable for life."

"I shouldn't be satisfied with five thousand dollars," said Peabody, whose ideas were lofty.

"How much would satisfy you?"

"About fifty thousand," said the young Bostonian, his face lighting up at the thought of so large a sum.

"And what would you do with it, if I may be so bold?" asked Ferguson.

"I would buy a nice house at the South End, furnish it handsomely, and live in style."

"I suppose you would marry?" suggested Tom smiling.

"I probably should," answered Peabody gravely.

"Perhaps you have already selected the lady."

"I have."

"Who is she?" asked John Miles. "Come, now, Peabody, don't be bashful."

"It is the daughter of a Boston merchant."

"Does the lady love you?"

"We understand each other," answered Peabody loftily. "She would marry me, poor as I am, but for her purse-proud, mercenary sire. It will be a happy day when, with my pockets full of gold, I enter his presence and claim his daughter's hand."

"I wish you success, Mr. Peabody," said Tom. "I hope you have no rivals."

"Yes, there is one."

"Are you not afraid of him?"

"Oh, no. He is a fellow of no style," said Peabody, drawing up his slender form and looking as stylish as a very dirty shirt, muddy boots, and a soiled suit would allow.

"I think I shall wait awhile before getting married," said Tom. "I am afraid I wouldn't stand any chance with an heiress, Mr. Peabody. Do you think I can ever be stylish?"

The Bostonian understood Tom to be in earnest and told him he thought in time, under proper training, he might become fairly stylish.

The conversation was interrupted by the ringing of a bell from the log house. Mrs. Fletcher, by an arrangement with the party, prepared their meals, and thus they fared better than most of the early pioneers. Their labor gave them a good appetite, and they were more solicitous about quantity than quality. Slow as he was at his work, there was no one who exhibited greater alacrity at meal-times, than Lawrence Peabody. At such times he was even cheerful.

BE SURE TO LISTEN TO THE AUDIOBOOK "STORIES OF SUCCESS" SERIES BY HORATIO ALGER, AVAILABLE ON AUDIBLE.COM AND ITUNES. GO TO WWW.SUMNERBOOKS.COM.

www.ingramcontent.com/pod-product-compliance
Lightning Source LLC
Chambersburg PA
CBHW071244130626
46556CB00003B/1157